Just Choose
Happiness

NELL W. MOHNEY

Just Choose Happiness

A Guide
to Joyous
Living

Abingdon Press / Nashville

Just Choose Happiness

This book is printed on acid-free paper.

Library of Congress Cataloging-in-Publication Data

Mohney, Nell.
   Just choose happiness : a guide to joyous living / Nell W. Mohney.
     p. cm.
   ISBN 978-0-687-64723-1 (pbk. : alk. paper)
   1. Happiness—Religious aspects—Christianity. I. Title.

   BV4647.J68M64 2009
   248.4—dc22

                        2008046398

09 10 11 12 13 14 15 16 17 18—10 9 8 7 6 5 4 3 2 1
MANUFACTURED IN THE UNITED STATES OF AMERICA

Contents

To my late husband,

Dr. Ralph Wilson Mohney, Sr.,

who brought me great happiness in this life,

and whose joyous commitment to Jesus Christ

gave me a foretaste of happiness in the world to come

Introduction

In seminars I have conducted over a thirty-year period, I have discovered that what the majority of people seem to want most is happiness. Many of those participants drove to the seminars in luxury cars, and they all looked well fed and well dressed. Yet, individually, they often expressed disappointment with life and admitted to having a feeling of emptiness. They wanted, and even felt entitled to, more happiness.

Many authors writing about this subject suggest that happiness is the result of maintaining good physical health and taking the right vitamins. Others equate happiness with how we think, or how much of the world's wealth we can amass. Of course, there is some truth in each of these approaches as part of the answer.

The cost of health care has risen to almost unmanageable proportions in part because we haven't learned to take care of our bodies. Also, the fact that one half of all hospital beds in the western world are occupied by people with emotional or mental illness indicates a need for transforming our minds (W. E. Sangster, *The Secret of Radiant Living* [Grand Rapids, Mich.: Zondervan, 1988], 7).

Additionally, the abject poverty in our world must grieve the heart of God. We as Christians must work for justice in political and economic systems, as well as learn to manage our own finances and develop the gift of generosity. Still, a full stomach, a healthy body and mind, and enough money to provide for necessities will not take the ache from the human soul.

I am one of those who truly believe that the basic answer to happiness is a spiritual one. We are made for God, and as St. Augustine said, "Our hearts are restless until they rest in Thee." All aspects of our personalities are drawn to wholeness and happiness when Christ is resident within.

In studying the life of Christ, I remembered anew that though Jesus was a man of sorrow and acquainted with grief, more than anything else, he was a person of joy and happiness. His last will and testament given to his disciples just before he died was this: "I have said these things to you so that my joy may be in you, and that your joy may be complete" (John 15:11).

Christ's purpose in coming into the world is revealed in John 10:10: "I came that they may have life, and have it abundantly." This abundant life, I believe, is to be had not only in the world to come but also in the here and now, where a series of committed choices can cause your spirit to sing.

We'll explore these committed choices—one in each chapter. There is a section at the end of each chapter entitled "Digging a Little Deeper" that can be used for individual reflection or group discussion, making the book appropriate for both individual and group study. May you find this small volume a guidebook to joyous, happy living.

CHAPTER ONE

Choose Life

I have set before you life and death, blessings and curses. Choose life so that you and your descendants may live. (Deuteronomy 30:19)

Tim, how can you be so happy when you live in excruciating pain?" I asked Dr. Tim Hansel in a conference I was attending. All of us were drawn to this handsome keynote speaker who illumined the words of life and Christian vitality with humor and persuasion. At each session, he threw a rope of hope to those of us who were struggling with ordinary, everyday problems. We left each session feeling that we were "more than conquerors through him who loved us" (Romans 8:37).

It was in a small social group following an evening session that we learned through the hostess that Tim had been seriously injured in a mountain-climbing expedition. For a while, doctors believed that Tim would not survive. He lived, but daily he faces excruciating pain. I had asked the question of Tim because I know it is one thing to be happy and have a sense of well-being when everything is going well; it is quite another when your body is wracked with pain.

When I asked the question, Tim put down his cup of tea, looked me directly in the eyes, and replied, "Every morning when I get up, I choose to be happy. You can choose to be happy, or you can choose to be miserable. I choose to be happy." Many years later, I heard another Christian author and speaker, Barbara Johnson, say similar words in a conference: "Pain is inevitable, but misery is a choice." I'd like to add, "And so is happiness."

Then Tim said, "If you think I am happy, you ought to know my friend Mark." He described his friend as a football coach at a western university and then added that Mark has no hands. He uses hooks, and he has become so adept at using them that he also plays tennis and rides a bike.

Tim told us that Mark sometimes takes off the hooks. When he encounters amazed stares or questions, Mark unselfconsciously responds with good humor and a happy, accepting attitude. For example, one day Tim accompanied Mark to the grocery store before they left to go to a church meeting. Because Mark didn't have on the hooks, he used both wrists to pick up the items and drop them into the grocery cart. At the cereal counter, two boys about six or seven years old watched in disbelief as Mark found his cereal of choice and used his wrists to transfer the box into the cart. Then came the inevitable question: "Mister, what happened to your hands?" Mark, in mock surprise, looked down and said, "Oh, my goodness, where are they? I must have left them up among the cereal boxes." The boys quickly joined in the search until Mark declared, "Now I remember." The boys asked in unison, "What?" Mark's fun reply was, "When I washed my hands this morning, I must have left them lying on the lavatory."

How would you handle the loss of both hands? Would it destroy your happiness and even lead to bitterness? That story confirmed for me the truth of this statement: What happens to you is not as important as your reaction to what happens to you. This was certainly true of the children of Israel when they left the slavery of Egypt to become a nation during their years in the wilderness, eventually moving into the Promised Land.

When the children of Israel were looking over into the Promised Land, God spoke to them through Moses: "I call heaven and earth to witness against you today that I have set before you life and death, blessings and curses. Choose life so that you and your descendants may live" (Deuteronomy 30:19).

Think of it. The Israelites wandered in the wilderness for forty years and finally were at the fulfillment of a dream, yet they were afraid and unsure that they had what was necessary to move into the challenge of a new lifestyle. God was telling them that they could stay in the shadows of fear and despondency (death of the spirit), or they could, in trust and faith, move forward toward life. God said, "Choose life."

Often we have an opportunity to move toward a new challenge, but we are afraid to move out of safe yet unhappy and deadening ruts. God must surely be saying to us, "Choose life." Will we heed the words or stay in the shadows? God has given us freedom of choice, and he will never bulldoze his way into our lives. The choice is ours. As Tim Hansel said during the conference I attended, "We choose happiness at the core of who we are when we invite Christ to live within us not only as Savior but also as Lord. We invite him in as King to reign forever, and not just as president to serve for a four-year term." This is the first step in choosing life and happiness—inviting Christ to live within us.

Are Your Flags Flying?

In 1984, my husband, Ralph, and I did a ministerial exchange in England. We thoroughly enjoyed our time there and loved the English people. Soon we discovered that when the Queen was in residence at Buckingham Palace, her flag flew above the palace. The apostle Paul tells us in Galatians 5:22-23 that when Christ is in residence within us, the following "flags" will be flying in our lives: love, joy, peace, patience, kindness, generosity, faithfulness, gentleness, and self-control.

These flags don't fly at full mast the moment we choose to invite Christ in. Rather, as we live daily in his presence and open every room of our lives to his loving presence, we feel a new sense of happiness and power. Living with Christ is very different from simply believing in him. As we more fully open our lives to Christ's presence, the flags increase and are more fully opened. For example, we have more peace, joy, and patience. We become kinder, gentler, more generous, more faithful, and more self-controlled.

When our sons were six and eight years old, Ralph was serving as a District Superintendent of the United Methodist Church in East Tennessee. My mother, who lived in a small town in North Carolina, was dying of cancer. Because my father was an invalid, Mother wanted to die at home. This was before Hospice had been established. So my sister, my brother, and I provided household help for them. Also, our doctor, a family friend, checked on her regularly.

As she grew worse, we each took a week away from our families and stayed with Mother and Dad. Sometimes I drove across the mountains of western North Carolina to be with them, and sometimes I went by bus. One Sunday evening after I finished preparing food for my family for a week and making sure that the children's clothes were ready for school and their homework was finished, Ralph took me to the bus station.

Only fourteen passengers were aboard on that cold and starless night. Among us were two young soldiers, who obviously had just completed boot camp and already were feeling lonely. At the first rest stop, they got off the bus and bought cheese crackers and sodas for each of us. As they handed out the snacks, they asked what we did and where we lived. (This was a time when neighborliness was "in" and fear of terrorists had not arrived yet.) When they came to me, I told them where I lived; and for them, that was like seeing an old friend. They lived only thirty miles away in another Tennessee town.

When I said that I was a homemaker married to a minister, the taller young man looked pleased and sat down across the aisle from me. He said very earnestly, "Then I want to ask you a question." He told me that his family members were Christian, but he was not. Still, he went to church with them every Sunday he was home. Always he saw the same two men, and they raised a serious question in his mind. Both men were professing Christians. One was very involved in church activities, but he never looked happy. Instead, he looked weary in well-doing. The young man said, "When I see him, I think, 'If that's what it means to be a Christian, then I don't want it.'" He continued, "The other man has had many problems in his life, but he is always at church and always looks happy. When I am around him, I feel as if a spring breeze is blowing through his life. I say, 'If that's what it means to be Christian, then I want it.'"

Then, with a sense of urgency in his voice, he asked, "If they are both Christians, what is the difference?" I opened my heart and mind and prayed for an answer, and I'm sure I received one because I had never thought of it before. Yet it's the very thing the New Testament tells us so clearly. "The difference in the two men," I replied, "is that one man works for Christ, but the other one lives with him."

That's what the incarnation means: "in Christ, God was reconciling the world to himself" (2 Corinthians 5:19). As Christ becomes resident in us through the Holy Spirit, we receive guidance and power. This, of course, is an incredible gift from God, but we must choose to receive the gift. As Mary Martin once sang on Broadway in *The Sound of Music*, "A bell is not a bell until you ring it; a song is not a song until you sing it." I'd like to add, "A gift is not a gift until you receive it."

The Secret of Authentic Happiness

In his classic book *The Secret of Radiant Living*, English author William E. Sangster describes the gift of incarnation as the secret of authentic happiness and radiant personality. He says that the people who have authentic happiness are usually ordinary persons who do extraordinary things. They are empowered! Sangster says this happens to people who say to Christ, "Abide with me," and really mean it, entertaining with gladness their Holy Guest.

Although Christians through the years have not definitively been able to distinguish between the Father, the Son, and the Holy Spirit, there are important reasons we think of this divine indwelling as the Son. Christ himself said, "The Father and I are one" (John 10:30). Also, his name was Emmanuel, meaning "God is with us" (Matthew 1:23). In any case, it is obvious that when we draw nearer to God through Christ, we know him as much as we humans can. Through Christ, we see God in a human setting, hear his words, and share his experiences.

Sangster believes that seeking happiness by itself—apart from Christ—is eventually fruitless. It is like reaching for the bloom on a peach without touching the peach or the tree. The following three circles show the difference between person-centered living and Christ-centered living:

1. The first circle represents an unbeliever. This person has self at the center of his or her life. Christ is definitely on the outside. He has never been invited to come inside.

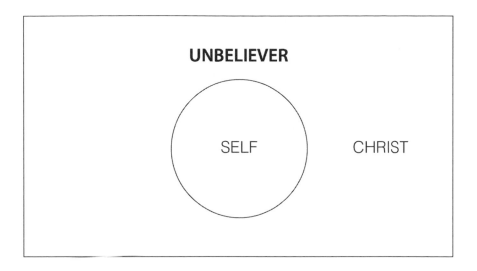

2. The second circle represents what Paul would call a carnal Christian and we would call a nominal Christian. That person may have received Christ as Savior, but none of the doors of the person's life is open to Christ's presence. The individual is still calling all the shots. Self is still at the center.

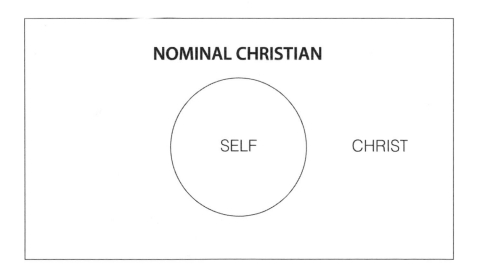

3. In the last circle, Christ has been invited to take up residence as Lord and King. All rooms are open, allowing changes to begin. Christ is at the

center of the life, and the self inside is being fulfilled to its potential. This is the spirit-filled Christian.

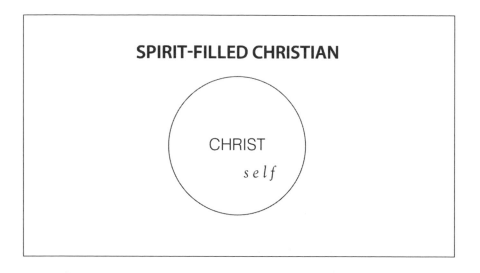

SPIRIT-FILLED CHRISTIAN

CHRIST

self

According to Sangster, the Spirit-filled life is the beginning of authentic and enduring happiness. The first thought of the Spirit-filled life is to recognize that we can't do it on our own. This means asking forgiveness for our mistakes and sins, accepting God's forgiveness, and then inviting Christ to live in every room of our lives as Lord. This also involves living in daily fellowship with Christ through prayer, Bible reading, quiet listening, and the willingness to follow his guidance.

Does that mean that we have nothing else to do once we have invited Christ into the center of our lives—that Christ will do it all? Absolutely not! The Spirit-filled life is a cooperative effort involving our growth not only in faith but also in the understanding that, as human beings, we are the totality of our thoughts, our feelings, and our will. Therefore, it is into the wholeness of our personalities that Christ must come and work. We can't merely learn through our minds what scientists, psychologists, and the Bible tell us about happiness—though we will do a bit of that learning in this book. We also must learn some things through intuition. For example, we intuitively know that kindness is better than cruelty and that truth is better than a lie. We also must learn through life experience and observation. It is in the totality of our personalities that Christ must live and work, just as it is in the fullness of him that "we live and move and have our being" (Acts 17:28).

A part of this cooperative effort involves choosing and developing positive and practical traits that will enhance our happiness. Among these are gratitude, kindness, laughter, forgiveness, time with family and friends, leaving old destructive habits behind, coping with stress and hardship, choosing fitness of body and mind, and living in the presence of Christ.

Sit back and enjoy the trip, but take it seriously; and you will emerge as a happy, growing Christian living in the flow of God's presence.

Digging a Little Deeper

1. According to this chapter, how do we establish a core foundation for happiness in life?
2. Respond to the following statement: What happens to you is not as important as your reaction to what happens to you. How have you experienced the truth of this statement in your own life?
3. How would you explain what it means to "Choose life"? Why does God leave this choice to us? Why do you think we are often afraid to choose life?
4. Read Deuteronomy 30:15-20. How is choosing life similar to choosing happiness? In what way do we "choose happiness at the core of who we are" when we invite Christ to live within us as Savior and Lord? How

is this *not* the same thing as saying that everything will always go well for us or that we will always be happy about every circumstance in our lives?

5. Read Galatians 5:22-23. According to these verses, what are the outward signs that Christ is in residence within us? Why don't these "flags" fly at full mast from the moment we invite Christ into our lives? How do they become more prevalent in our lives?

6. How is living with Christ different from believing in Christ? What are some of the ways you "live with Christ" each day?

7. Read John 15:1-5. What does it mean to abide in Christ? Why is this important?

8. Refer to the illustrations on pages 7–8. According to these representations, how would you explain the difference(s) between an unbeliever, a nominal Christian, and a Spirit-filled Christian?

9. Would you agree with William E. Sangster's assertion that allowing Christ to live and work in our lives is the basis for authentic and enduring happiness? Why or why not?

10. What does it mean to say that the Spirit-filled life is a cooperative endeavor? How can we cooperate with the indwelling presence of Christ?

CHAPTER TWO

Choose Gratitude

*Do not worry about anything, but in everything by
prayer and supplication with thanksgiving let your requests be
made known to God. And the peace of God, which surpasses
all understanding, will guard your hearts and your minds in
Christ Jesus. (Philippians 4:6-7)*

One of the most powerful secrets of happiness is gratitude. I am
convinced beyond a shadow of a doubt that gratitude opens our
hearts to life, to God, and to others; and ingratitude snaps our
hearts shut. Ingratitude produces whiners and complainers. Gratitude, on
the other hand, is an antidote for worry, stress, depression, and grief. It
enables us to become more balanced and gives us peace that "surpasses all
understanding" in the midst of chaos.

Throughout the psalms and the teachings of Jesus and Paul, the importance of gratitude as a means of grace is highlighted again and again. Even
so, it took me a long time to grasp the correlation between gratitude and
happiness.

Worry Leads to Discouragement and Depression

Maybe it is partially my temperament, as well as a tendency I have toward perfectionism, that made worry easy for me. Nevertheless, eventually worry became a habit. Thank goodness habits can be broken! For years, I felt that if I weren't worrying about something, I was not being practical. I realized that I was much like my friend's husband who actually awakened her in the middle of the night saying, "Don't just lie there—worry!"

Worry causes us always to expect the worst. When Ralph was late getting home, I became convinced that there had been an accident. I lived under a great cloud of anxiety. My stomach would churn, and my head would begin hurting. My thoughts simply couldn't focus on other things. My mind was like a broken record, playing the same fear over and over.

One incident helped me to face the pathetic reality of my situation. Our son and his friend, both age six, had climbed a small oak tree in our backyard. When I went outside and saw them, my worry became anxiety. "Rick, come down immediately. You may fall and break your leg." My son pleaded, "But Mom, we're finding the best place to build a tree house." With my heart racing and a vision of Rick lying immobile on a hospital bed, I said sternly, "Come down at once." As he reluctantly descended, he said that his friend's mother had stopped and said how proud she was of them for being able to climb so high.

Suddenly I saw how I might be passing on my fears and worries to my six-year-old. "Maybe I'm just being afraid," I said guiltily as I served Rick milk and cookies as an act of penance. Yet I knew that I needed help. First, I admitted my fears to God and asked for his help. Second, I began a study of what the Bible has to say about the importance of our thoughts, such as: "Let the same mind be in you that was in Christ Jesus"

(Philippians 2:5); "Do not be conformed to this world, but be transformed by the renewing of your minds, so that you may discern what is the will of God—what is good and acceptable and perfect" (Romans 12:2). I also studied what God's Word says about fear. I still repeat two of those verses often: "For God did not give us a spirit of cowardice, but rather a spirit of power and of love and of self-discipline" (2 Timothy 1:7) and "I can do all things through [Christ] who strengthens me" (Philippians 4:13). Most of all, I made a new commitment to faith in Christ. I realized that he didn't spend his life in worry, fear, and anxiety. He sought to do God's will, and he completely trusted God for the future.

My greatest breakthrough came when a circumstance over which I had no control devastated me. No amount of worry or pleading changed the situation. I felt I was powerless; I felt like a crumpled piece of paper in a room of disarray. It happened when a physician said to my husband, Ralph, and me: "I'm sorry, but the injuries were too great to sustain life. Your son is dead!" For a while, I became like a robot. I went through the motions of dressing, cooking, and going to the office, but life seemed surreal. It was as if I were standing on the outside, observing events on the inside. There seemed to be no feeling left in my body.

Fortunately, I maintained my habit of a daily quiet time with scripture reading and prayer. One day, a verse I had read many times before simply jumped off the page and shouted to me, "This is for you!" It was in Paul's first letter to the Thessalonians: "Give thanks in all circumstances; for this is the will of God in Christ Jesus for you" (5:18). God seemed to be saying to me, "Wake up. It's time to give thanks." I remonstrated by saying, "How can I give thanks when we have lost our firstborn child?" Yet I was convinced that God was saying, "Do it!"

I knew that God didn't cause my son's death, but I wanted desperately to hold onto the pre-accident past—to a fully alive twenty-year-old son.

Each time I started down that road, I seemed to hear in my mind God's words through Paul in 1 Thessalonians 5:18: "Give thanks in all circumstances." One day I awakened reluctantly, wanting to pull the covers over my head. I was tired and didn't want to give thanks, but gently and quietly God's voice came back to me, "Do it, Nell, and your pain will ease."

It has taken me time, self-discipline, and trust, but worry is no longer the centerpiece of my life. Thanks be to God!

Thanksgiving Overcomes Grief

The simple practice of giving thanks every day revolutionized my life, and I do it to this day each morning before I get out of bed. On the rare occasions when I oversleep, I am irritable with others and impatient with myself. At the time of Rick's death, my prayer went something like this:

> O God, in the midst of my pain, I thank you for a husband who loves me; for another son who is a blessing to our lives; for the twenty years we had Rick with us; for family and friends who support us; for a job that requires thought and action; for the church, the body of Christ, that has shown us your love in practical ways, pointing us constantly toward the real source of our help—God, Jesus Christ, and the Holy Spirit; and for your solid assurance that life doesn't end under six feet of earth. Thank you! Thank you! Thank you!

I can truthfully report that, day by day, my grief began to lift. Thanksgiving freed my mind to know joy again. It was then that I discovered the secret of happiness through thanksgiving. Now whenever life becomes too stressful, I take one full month in which I pray only prayers of thanksgiving. Then I am able to see life in a whole new perspective. Only then can I fully understand the hidden power of gratitude.

The Power of Gratitude

The New World Dictionary of American English defines gratitude as "a feeling of thankful appreciation for favors, for benefits received." Cicero, a Roman poet, philosopher, orator, and statesman who lived in the first century before Christ, said, "Gratitude is not only the greatest of virtues, but the parent of all others." In other words, gratitude is the ground on which every virtue rests. I'd like to suggest three reasons that this is true—three powerful ways that gratitude can affect every aspect of our lives.

1. Gratitude is life empowering

Gratitude can change the way you feel about yourself. As you regularly focus on, give thanks for, and use the gifts and talents God has given you, you overcome feelings of inferiority. Gratitude empowers you to appreciate what others are doing without feeling in competition with them. It moves you from a reactionary mode to taking charge of your life.

I have a friend for whom worry and negativism have become a way of life. Earlier in her life, she was an excellent portrait artist. A very difficult divorce and resultant financial problems left her fragmented and over-whelmed. Replaying the difficult circumstances became so habitual that rather than forming a practical plan of action, she would react in despair and place blame on others. Recently, a group of Christian friends have helped her in many ways, enabling her to focus on her blessings and return to Sunday school and church and a faith that will hold her. These friends are truly being the body of Christ for her.

2. Gratitude increases your energy

Imagine yourself in the center of a big balloon. When you experience gratitude, your balloon is full and expanded. You feel alive and healthy,

15

and you are a healing presence. But when you are complaining or having negative thoughts and fears, your balloon begins to deflate. You feel drained, out of sorts, heavy, and without vitality. Your energy has leaked away.

Recently, when I told a friend about this book and said that I needed an illustration about gratitude and energy, she told me of an incident in her own life. She was feeling overwhelming gratitude for a grandson who had graduated from college with honors. He had experienced learning disabilities since early childhood, so his graduation and the offer of a good job were almost too good to be true. She felt not only grateful for answered prayer but also very alive and energetic. Shortly, however, she learned that her neighbor had not received the part she wanted in a Little Theater production. She allowed the bad news to deflate her balloon of gratitude and throw her into the slough of despond. The choice is ours!

3. Gratitude improves the quality of your life

There's no doubt about it: The quality of our lives depends upon what we focus on. The practice of focusing on gratitude and expressing it will amplify, enrich, and empower your life. The key word is *practice*. Gratitude requires practice and discipline.

Just this week, I read of a man who was in Manhattan in the late sixties and needed directions to Carnegie Hall. He saw what was then called a "hippie" with a guitar hung over his shoulder. The visitor rolled down his car window and asked, "How do I get to Carnegie Hall?" Without even slowing down, the hippie replied, "Practice, man, practice." We need to develop the practice of focusing on gratitude.

Have you ever greeted someone with the simple question "How are you?" and received as a reply an "organ recital"? You know, the person rehearses every part of the anatomy that hurts and includes the details of the surgeries he or she has had, as well as the bad news the doctor has given. You finally get away from the person, but you feel drained, exhausted, and unhappy. Interestingly, the individual feels even worse but continues painting the sad picture for anyone who will listen. This person hasn't learned the secret of choosing gratitude.

When you focus on things for which you are grateful, you unleash power to become more and more the person God created you to be.

Jesus Acknowledged the Power of Gratitude

In Luke 17:11-19, the Gospel writer tells a simple but poignant story of ten lepers who cried out to Jesus for healing as he passed through a village in Samaria. Remember that leprosy in that day was a fate worse than death. There was no cure for this contagious and mutilating disease.

At that time, when persons realized that they had the disease, they were required to leave their homes, families, and businesses and go to a leper colony, often living in caves outside the city. When they came within twenty feet of a person who didn't have the disease, the lepers had to call out in a loud voice, "Unclean! Unclean!" It was the most dreaded disease not only because of the terrible physical mutilation but also because of the loneliness and humiliation caused by the exclusion from normal society. Naturally, the lepers longed to be healed.

When the lepers heard that Jesus was approaching the village of which they once had been respected citizens, they cried out from a distance their desire to be made whole: "Jesus, Master, have mercy on us!" (v. 13). Jesus told them to go show themselves to the priests, and they would be healed. As they went, they were cleansed and made whole. One of them returned to thank Jesus and to glorify God. Jesus asked, "Were not ten made clean? But the other nine, where are they?" (v. 17).

As a young person, I didn't understand Jesus' question. Did he just want to be recognized for his ability to heal? Was he trying to teach the men about social graces—about the elemental skill of saying "Thank you"? I am convinced that it was neither of these reasons. Jesus knew that gratitude blessed the person who expressed it far more than the person to whom it was expressed. He knew that gratitude is the key to vitality and power, as well as the key to happiness.

Gratitude Overcomes Depression

Gratitude also allows us to overcome a feeling of depression.

Years ago, I was privileged to accompany my husband, Ralph, when he served as a college president, as he visited European universities. We met with chancellors and with faculty and student groups at universities that were as diverse as Oxford and Cambridge and those in the communist countries such as East Germany and the Soviet Union. Our last stop was in Zurich, Switzerland. When I awakened on the last day of our trip, I suddenly realized that we had been so busy with our meetings that I had had no time to shop for promised gifts for our two children. So I skipped the meetings and went to a charming little shop.

As I browsed, I saw a most unusual walking stick. It was highly polished with a handsome brass handle and unusual carvings on either side. On the left side, there were three large notches—and more notches than I could count on the right side. The owner saw me examining the stick and said abruptly, "That's not for sale." Curious about it, I asked, "Will you tell me about it?"

Looking at me as if to decide whether or not to trust me, he put down some merchandise and said, "That's my gratitude stick." Then he told me how he had experienced three devastating events in four years and had become very depressed. The first was when his gift shop had burned to the ground. That in itself was difficult with the loss of income for him and his employees. He did, however, have a good insurance policy, and workmen were available to rebuild the shop even bigger than before— and rather quickly. Though this discouraged him, it was the next two events that traumatized him since they came within months of each other. One was the death of one of his three sons. The sixteen-year-old boy was handsome and intelligent, and he had plans to enter medical school. His was a senseless killing by a drunken driver. The shop owner was disconsolate; but with the help of his wife and the parish priest, he was just beginning to come out of that valley of grief when he learned that his business partner had embezzled a large sum of money from the gift shop and had left Zurich.

It was the proverbial straw that broke the camel's back. His discouragement turned to despair and then to deep depression. He became so ill that he could not function in his work or personal life. Meditation and prayer helped. But it was a simple technique used by his wife that seemed to bring him back to normalcy. She handed him two sheets of blank paper. One was entitled "Bad Things That Happened to Me." On that paper, he listed the three traumas that had brought him to the very core of his existence. Then he looked at the second sheet. It was entitled "Things for Which I Am Grateful." As he began to write, one after another came to mind more quickly than he could write:

1. A loving wife and her patience with me.
2. Two healthy sons who have fine characters and great plans for the future.
3. A sure knowledge that our son who died is in heaven and that we will see him again.
4. A Christian faith that holds me steady in the midst of pain and problems.
5. Church members and friends who surround us with love and care.
6. The opportunity to live in the shadow of our beloved Alps, where we see the beauty of God's creation.
7. A new shop that is doing well despite my absence.

He continued to write until he had listed over twenty things for which he was grateful. As he wrote, the heaviness in his heart began to lessen so that he could tackle life again.

His wife suggested that he make a gratitude stick. On the left side, he made notches for the traumas he had experienced. On the right side, there were more notches representing the things for which he was grateful. He said, "When I begin to feel discouraged, I rub the right side of my stick and remember and count my blessings."

Since that experience, I always keep an imaginary gratitude stick nearby to count my blessings at the first thought of discouragement. It works for me, and I challenge you to try it.

A Gratitude List That Will Make You Think

A friend sent me an unusual and thought-provoking gratitude list that has been widely circulated in various forms. The list described more than a dozen of what I call "hidden blessings," and it prompted me to write my own list. Here it is:

I am thankful . . .

For a husband who loved and encouraged me for almost sixty years.

For the Resurrection, which assures me that my husband and son are at home with Christ in heaven.

For a son, daughter-in-law, and grandchildren, who bring only joy and delight into my life. I'm enormously thankful that each one, including our grandson-in-law, is a joyful follower of the Galilean.

For friends, both new and old and far and near, who have brought me comfort and help during the illness and death of my husband. They, also, have continuously pushed me into the future.

For a Sunday school class of singles that I have the privilege of teaching. They have found so many practical ways in which to demonstrate God's unconditional love.

For my church, which lifts up Christ and challenges its members to be servant leaders.

For my country, which, though it faces formidable obstacles, still gives us hope for the future.

For a two-party system that gives our government balance.

For the gift of life and the opportunity to move with God into his future.

Let me suggest that you make your own gratitude list. When you are discouraged, feel sorry for yourself, or are tempted to whine or complain or be negative, bring out your gratitude list and realize how blessed you are.

Digging a Little Deeper

1. How would you define *gratitude*?

2. In what ways does ingratitude close your heart? How can gratitude open your heart—to life, to God, and to others?

3. Worry often causes our thoughts to go round and round like a broken record, keeping us from taking constructive action. What other bad effects of worry have you experienced?

4. Read Philippians 4:6-7. What does Paul say is the antidote for worry? How is thanksgiving to be a part of the process?

5. Read 1 Thessalonians 5:18. What does this verse tell us to do? What is the difference between giving thanks *for* all things and giving thanks *in* all things?

6. Have you ever had a sense of powerlessness as I did when our son died? Share as you are comfortable. How has obeying the words of 1 Thessalonians 5:18 helped you to overcome times of grief, fear, or worry?

7. What does it mean to say that gratitude is "powerful"?

8. How can gratitude change the way we feel about ourselves and empower us?

9. How can gratitude increase our energy and vitality?

10. How can gratitude improve our quality of life?

11. Read Luke 17:11-19. Why do you think Jesus was concerned about the nine lepers who had been healed but failed to give thanks?

12. Think of a time when you felt and expressed gratitude. How was this a blessing to you?

13. How did the shopkeeper in Zurich overcome his depression? What lesson can we learn from him?

14. Right now, begin making a list of things for which you are most grateful. This list will help to enable you to overcome the temptation to complain or allow grief and depression to overcome you.

CHAPTER THREE

Choose Not to Live in the Past

Then the LORD said to Moses, "Why do you cry out to me? Tell the Israelites to go forward." (Exodus 14:15)

Every school day during my high school years, I had to pass a haunted house on my way to school. Actually, it was a large old mansion that once had been the scene of glittering parties described as the social events of the year in that North Carolina town. Stories were told of the governor and his wife, other state officials, and a U.S. Senator who lived in our town and would arrive at the parties in chauffeur-driven limousines.

When the master of the house, who owned the town's largest industry, died suddenly of a heart attack, his widow went into mourning—and never came out! The house, which once had been so full of life and laughter, now had all the blinds drawn tight. Even when a light was on, the mansion still looked dark. The widow left the house only for a visit to the doctor's office or an occasional errand. She always wore black and looked sad. Her earlier vivacity was no longer apparent. She was stuck in the past.

Other people stay stuck in the past because of happy memories. Harold, an automobile salesman, lived with his wife and two children across the street from my family. He was a jovial man who loved to talk, and his conversation always centered around his one claim to fame. He had made the touchdown that won the state championship for our high school football team. That had happened twenty years earlier, but he couldn't talk with anyone for five minutes without weaving in his victory. Like the widow, Harold was stuck in the past.

Memory Is a Wonderful Gift

Memory truly is a wonderful gift. We can sit comfortably in our homes and remember events that happened when we were five, ten, or sixteen years old. If we are older, we can remember funny incidents that happened in courtship, early marriage, or the parenting days. Yes, the past is a wonderful place to visit for happy memories, and it is a place where we can learn from our mistakes. Yet we must never live there!

One of the benefits of remembering the past is getting a clear perspective of God's guidance in our lives in good times and bad. During my junior year in college, several things were not working out in my career plans as I had hoped. For one thing, I became ill and missed a big interview for a position I really wanted. To make matters worse, I had been elected president of a campus-wide student organization, and their annual installation ceremony was a big event. I had purchased a beautiful long dress for the occasion. One day before the installation, a tragic event happened on campus that cancelled all activities, even classes. I was discouraged! When I called home, my dad listened understandingly and then said, "When I get discouraged, I hold on to my highest moments."

"What does that mean?" I asked. Then I said in a disgruntled voice that I felt my tragedies were being marginalized. My dad replied, "I remember the many times God has been there for me and how well things eventually worked out, and I give thanks." That simple formula gave me an immediate, clear picture. It worked for me then, and it has worked for me many times since. "Hold on to your high moments" is the formula that has allowed me to deal with both the little disappointments, such as the ones I have mentioned (though they seemed huge to me at the time), and the big, very real tragedies.

God has created three "time slots": past, present, and future. We learn from the past and trust God for the future, but we live only in the present. God calls us to live fully in the present and move expectantly toward the future—not to get stuck in the past. The story of the Israelites' exodus from Egypt makes this abundantly clear.

God Called the Israelites to Go Forward

The children of Israel had been slaves in Egypt under Pharaoh. It was a miserable existence, but they were habituated to it. Still, they knew that God had fulfilled his promise when he sent Moses to rescue them—to say to the Pharaoh, "Let my people go." It must have been awesome to watch Pharaoh withstand such plagues as water turned to blood, frogs, gnats, flies, diseased livestock, boils, hail, locusts, and darkness (Exodus 7–10). The Pharaoh finally agreed to let the Israelites go when the angel of death passed over the homes of the Israelites to attack the firstborn in every Egyptian home, including the palace.

As the approximately two million Israelites journeyed out of the familiar into the unknown, they must have experienced exhilaration at the thought of freedom and anxiety as they faced the great unknown. Then they came to the dramatic moment when they stood before the threatening waters of the Red Sea while hearing the approaching chariots of Pharaoh's army. Pharaoh had changed his mind! The entire economic structure of Egypt would be decimated by the loss of that many slaves. As the Israelites looked at the sea before them and heard Pharaoh's chariots behind them, they must have felt trapped. Either way, surely they would experience death and destruction. Then God spoke through Moses: "Tell the Israelites to go forward." Remember that they were asked to step into the sea *before* the waters parted. It had to be an act of faith demonstrating their trust in God.

We know the rest of the story. The Israelites stepped into the water, Moses raised his staff, and the waters parted so that the Hebrew people could walk safely out of Egyptian territory. The waters came back together only when the Egyptians tried to cross on dry land. Pharaoh's army disappeared in the waters of the Red Sea.

I like the story of the mother who, on the way home from church, asked her eight-year-old son, Jimmy, what he had learned in Sunday school that morning. "Oh, Mama, it was great!" Jimmy answered. "Our teacher told us about Moses leading the children of Israel out of Egypt. Before they reached the Red Sea, Moses picked up his walkie-talkie and told the engineers to build a pontoon bridge over the sea. When the Hebrews walked across the pontoon bridge, then Moses called the bombardiers, telling them to blow up the bridge; and all the Egyptians were killed."

"Jimmy, is that really what the teacher told you?" asked his mother. The eight-year-old lowered his head and said, "No, Mama, but if I told you what she told us, you would never believe it."

To be sure, the biblical story of what happened to the Israelites at the Red Sea and in the wilderness has something to teach us.

What the Israelites Teach Us

1. We can be happy despite our circumstances

The truly great Christians I have known and read about have been happy people. Yet, like the Israelites, each of these persons faced a life-or-death situation. How were they able to be happy? They lived with the assurance that Christ is with us and will never leave us or forsake us (Hebrews 13:5).

I think of Corrie Ten Boom, for example. Before World War II, she lived with her parents and siblings in their home in Haarlem, Holland. When the Nazis came to Holland, Corrie and her family felt that it was their duty to help their Jewish friends. They hid them in the Ten Boom home or helped them to escape by leaving the city. The Ten Booms were arrested by the Gestapo and sent to different concentration camps in Germany. Corrie's brother and her sister, Betsy, died in the camps. For years after her sister's death, Corrie Ten Boom spoke to Christian audiences about her experiences in a concentration camp and the awesome power of forgiveness. Corrie obviously would have agreed with John Wesley, the founder of Methodism, who reportedly said just before he died, "The best of it is, God is with us" ("Famous Last Words," Answers.com).

The Israelites found they had to trust God for everything. They received food (manna) each morning (Exodus 16:14-26) and water that had been sweetened (Exodus 15:24-25). They found God faithful and trustworthy. We, despite our circumstances, can learn to do the same thing, knowing that God's promises are true.

2. Christ can heal our broken hearts

Life has a way of knocking us down and often breaking our hearts. As a minister's wife, I have observed hearts broken over the death of a loved

29

one, an unwanted divorce, broken engagements, financial disasters, extramarital affairs, a long, lingering illness, betrayal by a business partner, rebellion of a teenager, substance abuse on the part of a family member, and many other situations.

Some people try to heal their own brokenness without allowing Christ to be the Great Physician and allowing others to help. Most of these persons become bitter or harsh, or seek to escape their circumstances through drugs, alcohol, sexual promiscuity, or some other destructive behavior.

My experience is that we need to remember that Christ can heal us only when we walk daily with him by pouring out our hearts in prayer and reading the Scriptures to remember God's promises and how much God loves us. Gratitude for what we have left is an important component in this healing process.

The waters of the future may look deep and foreboding, and your anxiety level may be high; but hear God say to you as he did to the Hebrew people: "Tell [your name] to go forward." Only then can you move gently into a new day and know joy and deep happiness again.

3. God is always with us, acting on our behalf

When Moses asked what God's name was, God answered, "I AM WHO I AM" (Exodus 3:14).

Indeed, God is not the great "I Was" or the great "I Will Be." God is the great "I Am." God's mercies are new every day. He gives us direction for life through the Bible and through the Holy Spirit—in the "now" time slot, not in the past.

The Israelites must have found God to be the "Great I Am" when God parted the waters of the Red Sea, provided food and water in the wilderness, gave them the Ten Commandments, and finally brought them into the Promised Land.

Certainly God is for us "a very present help" in time of trouble (Psalm 46:1). God's presence in our worship and in our reading of the Word gives us encouragement when we're despairing, hope when we are fearful, peace when we are in the midst of storms, and joy when we are growing weary on our journey. The apostle Paul said in Philippians 3:13-14: "Beloved, I do not consider that I have made it my own; but this one thing I do: forgetting what lies behind . . . I press on toward the goal for the prize of the heavenly call of God in Christ Jesus." Unless we, like the Israelites and the apostle Paul, allow God to minister to us in the now, we will stay stuck in the past.

If *You* Are Stuck in the Past . . .

1. Receive God's forgiveness

You may be stuck in the past because you haven't received God's forgiveness of past mistakes and sins. Perhaps you do not feel worthy of moving into the newness that God has prepared for you. One of my favorite Bible verses is Isaiah 43:19: "I am about to do a new thing; now it springs forth, do you not perceive it? I will make a way in the wilderness and rivers in the desert." If you feel past sins and mistakes are keeping you from experiencing the freedom and newness that God has prepared for you, then you need to confess your sins, sincerely seek God's forgiveness, and *accept it with gratitude*.

My friend Catherine is one of the most attractive and radiant Christians I know. She and her husband were married for thirty years and had two beautiful children. The four of them were supportive of one another, active in their church, and had daily devotions together—even by telephone when her husband was traveling. It devastated Catherine and the children and rocked the community when her husband decided to end the marriage.

In the midst of her terrible pain, Catherine allowed Christ to heal her broken heart and enable her to forgive her husband. She remained strong for the children and was an inspiration to all who knew her.

From experience, I know that when you practice forgiveness and accept God's forgiveness, you feel as if a great weight has been lifted off your shoulders. Your entire body will feel lighter and your spirit will begin to sing again. That is a recipe for happiness:

> Confession (Repentance) + Acceptance of God's Forgiveness = Peace and Happiness.

2. Let go of resentment

You may be carrying resentment in your heart against someone who has hurt you. Even if you are justified in that feeling, resentment will eat you alive. In his book *Seizing the Moments*, James W. Moore tells of a woman who was dying of her inability to digest food. Specialists had given her every conceivable test and could find nothing physically wrong with her. They called her minister to see if he could determine whether or not there was an emotional cause for this strange occurrence. There was!

In the early years of her marriage, her husband had had a brief affair with a neighbor after they had moved to a new city. The wife had completely forgiven her husband, but she carried a deep grudge against the other woman. In fact, she had said to the minister, "I'd like to tear her limb from limb." The minister helped the woman understand that the resentment, buried deeply within her mind, was actually killing her physically. He gave her some books on overcoming resentment and pointed out how resentment actually keeps us tied to the person whom we resent.

Being an intelligent woman, she quickly recognized that she was self-destructing. She began to understand why Jesus was so insistent about the necessity of forgiving others and the freeing power this brings. When she was fully able to forgive the woman, instead of remaining stuck in the past, she immediately overcame her inability to digest food. The following Sunday, she returned to church, waving radiantly to her doctor across the sanctuary.

Jesus was a master psychologist. He knew that resentment is like having a splinter in your finger. If it is not removed, it will cause infection and pain. Though his teachings often appear difficult, they are a key to health and happiness.

3. Keep looking ahead

In Genesis 19:15-26, we find the story of Lot and his wife leaving the wicked city of Sodom. God commanded that they not look back at the destruction. When Lot's wife looked back, she turned into a pillar of salt.

Once I was telling this story to a group of inner-city children. When I said, "Lot's wife looked back and turned into a pillar of salt," a little boy raised his hand. "What is it, Mark?" I asked. He replied, "My mama looked back in the back seat to see what we were doing, and she turned into a telephone pole."

We won't turn into a pillar of salt or a telephone pole when we are stuck in the past, but we won't become what God is calling us to be.

Refusing to turn loose of the past can be just as disastrous to us as it was to Lot's wife. We may not die physically, but we die to receiving God's forgiveness and God's plans for us today.

I know of a man whose alcoholism cost him his family. He has been to rehab and has been sober for four years, but he has refused to accept God's forgiveness and forgive himself. He torments himself with guilt and, unless he can change, will likely escape again into alcoholism.

Similarly, all of us who look to the past rather than to what lies ahead are destined to remain stuck. Those of us who have lost loved ones, for example, are familiar with the "if only" period that prevents us from moving forward in the grieving process. In the death of our son, Rick, I thought of all the mistakes I had made as a parent. In my rational mind, I knew that I had nothing to do with the accident that caused his death. Maybe it was my guilt at still being alive when someone so much younger had died. Thankfully, it was in my daily quiet time, as I read God's Word and prayed, that I felt the amazing presence of the Holy Spirit just as Jesus had promised. I had the assurance of God's love and forgiveness and the sure knowledge that I will see Rick again. It was that experience, plus all the gratitude I still had, that enabled me to move beyond my grief into the future that God had for me.

God has a future of hope for each one of us (Jeremiah 29:11). Let us keep looking ahead!

Digging a Little Deeper

1. We have only to look through a picture album and remember the happy times of the past to understand the gift of memory. Recall and share with the group one of your happiest memories.

2. Read Exodus 14:15. Why do you think God asked the Israelites to move forward *before* the waters of the Red Sea parted? When has God called you to take a step of faith, demonstrating your trust in him? What happened?

3. Have you ever been stuck in the past, even for a short period of time, because of grief, fear, resentment, or even victorious accomplishments? In what ways might you have been afraid or reluctant to trust God? If studying with a small group, take turns answering these questions. If studying alone, write your answers in a journal or notebook.

4. What does it mean to walk in faith under the direction of the Holy Spirit? How does this give us a sense of confidence and peaceful happiness?

5. How is it possible to be happy despite difficult circumstances? Have you experienced this?

6. Have you ever experienced Christ's healing of your broken heart or known someone who has experienced this? If so, share with the group.

7. Have you experienced God acting on your behalf, such as sending a person to bring encouragement or providing a book or sermon or newspaper column to bring the guidance you needed? Explain.

8. Read Isaiah 43:19. In what ways can ruts become comfortable to us? Why do you think we're often hesitant to move out of a rut and recognize the new thing that God is seeking to do in our lives?

9. What new thing do you sense God is doing in your life—or desiring to do? It may be in your personal life, your family life, your church life, your friendships, your finances, or some other area.

10. Has the inability to forgive someone ever had a stranglehold on your life? What were the causes and effects of this resentment?

11. In the Lord's Prayer, Jesus taught us to pray, "forgive us our sins, just as we have forgiven those who have sinned against us" (Matthew 6:12

NLT). Why is it necessary for us to forgive others in order to receive forgiveness? What can we do to clear the channel for God's forgiveness?

12. Like Lot's wife, have you ever focused too much on the past, or held on to old grudges, disappointments, or fears—consequently missing God's mercy and help in the present? Explain.

CHAPTER FOUR

Choose to Live Today

This is the day that the LORD has made; let us rejoice
and be glad in it. (Psalm 118:24)

Too many people postpone happiness. They say things such as, "I'll be happy when . . . my children are out of college; . . . we can buy our own home; . . . we have a larger house or car or boat; . . . we can retire." Other people use the "if only" theme. "I'd be happy if only . . . we had more money; . . . I'd received the job I deserve; . . . my adult children treated me better; . . . my spouse were still living." These people are making circumstances the determinant of happiness. The truth is that all of us know people who have what we would call "the good life" but who are miserable.

Once my husband, Ralph, and I were invited to accompany a couple to Florida for a meeting the two husbands would be attending. We flew to Ft. Lauderdale, Florida, on the couple's private jet. I remember thinking, *I could get used to this*, as we were served a marvelous lunch on board and our every need was supplied.

After arriving in Ft. Lauderdale, we boarded the couple's large yacht to meet the crew who would be sailing us to the islands after the meeting

was over. Some of the staff would keep the boat in spit-and-polish condition while the chef and his assistants would cook and serve our meals
after leaving port. While in port, we ate breakfast aboard the ship and
most other meals in exotic restaurants in Ft. Lauderdale and Miami.

One day, as my friend and I were basking in the early March sunshine
on the top deck, I thought, *This is truly the way to live.* She interrupted my
reverie when she confided, "I know that most people think I have everything that makes for happiness, but I am miserable." I was stunned as she
continued to tell me why this was true.

When I told Ralph about the conversation later, we both recalled
the summer we had met. After attending a World Conference of
Christian Youth in Oslo, Norway, we had joined three other American
youth to work for two months with our denomination's missionaries in
Poland. We were there to help in their program rehabilitating Polish
youth following World War II. Many of these Polish youth had lost
family members during the war; some had seen them shot down in cold
blood by the Nazis. Following the war, they were living under the
oppressive regime of Communist Russia, yet they were full of hope and
joy and were optimistic about their future. When the Russians would
not allow us to have a Bible, the Polish youth said, "They can make us
bury God no deeper than our hearts." I remembered those words decades
later when Pope John Paul II returned to his native land and millions
of Christians, both Catholic and Protestant, greeted him in a new and
free Poland.

What is the happiness differential between those Polish youth and my
wealthy friend? As I analyzed their situations carefully, I concluded that
the differential wasn't the amount of money they had. I've known rich
people who were very happy and poor people who were miserable.
Though I believe that we must do all we can to overcome poverty,

poverty itself is not the cause of unhappiness. No, the difference was that the Polish youth had a very deep trust in God that had been hammered out on the anvil of pain and suffering. God had sustained and strengthened them in the tragedy of war, and this enabled them to feel confident about the future. They had experienced God's love in powerful and profound ways.

Those youth had learned to live in the "now" time slot. They didn't dwell on their sufferings of the past but celebrated the blessings of the present. They fully trusted God for the future instead of worrying about and being fearful of what might lie ahead. They had learned the secret of living one day at a time.

Happy People Live One Day at a Time

In the sixteenth chapter of Exodus, we read how God fed the children of Israel in the wilderness one day at a time. When they awakened each morning, after the dew had lifted, the landscape looked as if it were covered with hoarfrost. As far as the eye could see, the ground was covered with small, white wafers that tasted as if they had been sweetened with honey. They called it manna. Each man was told to collect an omer (three quarts) of manna for each person in his tent. If they tried to collect enough for two days, the leftover portion would be spoiled by the second day. God meant for them to trust him one day at a time.

The only time that they could gather a double portion of manna was on the sixth day so that they didn't have to toil on the Sabbath. The extra portion they collected on that day never spoiled. In addition to manna in the morning, quail covered the land at dusk each evening so that the Israelites had both meat and bread.

It was in the terrible and stressful days of World War II that Dr. William Ousler, an English surgeon, used the story of manna from heaven in an address to medical students at Johns Hopkins University. He understood the stress under which those students were working. Many of them had friends who had been killed during the war. Others were torn between continuing their medical studies and quitting and serving in the war effort. It was in that setting that Dr. Ousler asked the young men and women to learn the art of living in what he called "day-tight compartments." In other words, he was saying they should study and learn from the past, trust God for the future, but live one day at a time.

Happy People Live with Enthusiasm

A while ago, Ralph and I attended a church where, twenty years earlier, Ralph had served as senior pastor. We were there for me to teach at a special anniversary of an adult Sunday school class I had organized years before. We had a delightful time greeting and visiting over one hundred members of the class who were present.

Afterward, we attended one of the church's three morning worship services. The congregation participated lustily in reciting the Apostles' Creed and Lord's Prayer and in singing the Gloria Patri and various familiar hymns. When it was time for the sermon, we were united as a Christian community.

I was eager to listen to the pastor, who happened to be an African American man serving an all-white congregation. He was speaking on one of the hardest parts of the Gospel: giving. He delivered the message with such passion, humor, and sincerity that you could actually feel how we were all being motivated to give more of ourselves and our resources for God's Kingdom purposes. He elicited a number of "Amens" from that cosmopolitan and sophisticated audience. It was exciting! I left thinking, *I don't know what he has, but I want it.*

At a luncheon later that day, I observed the minister's interactions with the guests and decided that he looked as if he had an inner fire. *That's it!* I thought. *It's enthusiasm.* Actually, the word "enthusiasm" comes from the Greek word *entheos,* meaning "God in us." Whether we call this Source by the name of God, Christ, or the Holy Spirit, they are the one and only Holy One.

I like to begin each day with my own paraphrase of the J. B. Phillips translation of Colossians 1:27: "The secret is this, [I insert my name here], Christ alive in you, bringing with him the hope of glorious things to come." During the day when I encounter a difficult person or situation, I remember that I am not alone; Christ lives in me. And I find that my old feelings of negativism and inferiority disappear. Using Philippians 4:13 as another affirmation each morning, I feel empowered and confident— even enthusiastic. For years, I thought that enthusiasm belonged only to those sanguine or sunny dispositions. Now I know that whatever our temperaments, if we know that the God of the universe lives within us, we can live with patience and zest.

I've also discovered that, although each of us receives the Holy Spirit at baptism, too many people consider this a past event and live their lives totally under their own direction. The persons who walk daily in the presence of Christ, seeking guidance from his Spirit within, are the ones who have contagious enthusiasm.

At a seminar I attended, business guru Tom Peters said, "If I have two people of equal qualifications who apply for a position, I will always choose the one who has enthusiasm because he or she will be self-motivated and will motivate others."

The famous historian Arnold Toynbee gave a specific plan for developing enthusiasm. He said, "Apathy can only be overcome by enthusiasm, and enthusiasm can only be aroused by two things: first, an ideal that takes the imagination by storm, and second, a definite intelligible plan for carrying that ideal into practice."

I believe the difference between enthusiasm and faith is very slight. In fact, my definition of enthusiasm is "faith that has been set on fire." This means that we should never be mentally lazy. As the apostle Paul writes, we should "do [our] best to present [ourselves] to God as one[s] approved by him . . . worker[s] who [have] no need to be ashamed" (2 Timothy 2:15). Then we allow the Holy Spirit to set us on fire with power.

On my birthday each year, I remind myself of the words of Henry David Thoreau: "None are so old as those who have outlived enthusiasm." I challenge you to experience the thrill of living by practicing enthusiasm—and living with hope.

Happy People Live with Hope

In preparation for writing this chapter, I spent several weeks in settings as varied as social events, family reunions, church meetings, and private conversations. In addition, I listed ten people whom I consider happy and ten who, in my opinion, are less than happy. After much reflection, I realized the big differential between the two groups: the unhappy people give in too easily to discouragement and despair, whereas the happy people understand the power of hope.

A tragic accident happened in our city several years ago. Two doctors and their handsome, talented, well-liked high school son were out in a boat on a vacation trip. Their son, Austin, had been water skiing behind the boat. After a refreshment break, they were ready to go again. The mother was driving the boat. Thinking that her son was still at the side, she put the boat in reverse. Unfortunately, Austin was behind the boat and immediately had both legs amputated above his knees. Can you imagine the horror and guilt that mother felt?

Austin was airlifted to a very fine hospital, was given the best medical care, and was later fitted with prostheses; and after several months, he returned to school. He continued in his leadership roles, was a valuable member of the school's winning golf team, and graduated with his class. Realizing that many young people do not have the financial resources available to them that he has, Austin has established a foundation to enable such youth to have money for the best rehabilitation.

When I asked Austin and his mother what got them through the accident and gave them hope for the future, both mentioned two things: strong family love and strong Christian faith. The mother said, "We worship a God of faithfulness and hope. In every difficulty, he provides a way out." As I left them, I thought of Hebrews 6:19: "Hope [is] a sure and steadfast anchor of the soul."

In my own experience of having two surgeries for ovarian cancer and ten months of chemotherapy, I discovered that my hope comes from trusting God. I knew that either way—whether I lived or whether I died—I could trust God with my future. What greater hope can we have than this?

Through the years, leaders in almost every endeavor have affirmed the value and potency of hope. In his classic work *Walden*, Henry David Thoreau suggests that hope allows us to grasp the future. He writes, "I learned this by my experiment, that if one advances confidently in the direction of his dreams, and endeavors to live that life which he has imagined, he will move with success unexpected in common hours."

Studies conducted by psychologists in recent years confirm that hope plays a significantly important role in helping people to overcome and succeed—from academic endeavors to difficult jobs to difficult life situations and tragedies.

God Is Our Best Hope

By regularly reading God's word, praying, and worshiping, by walking daily with Christ, and by associating with positive Christians, we can cultivate and hold onto hope.

When discouragement or despair seems to have a hold on us, God is our best hope. In times of temptation and difficulty, God holds us steady, draws us toward his goals, and enables us to walk confidently and happily into the next dimension of life. What a powerful difference hope can make in our lives!

Biblical affirmations are a powerful way to strengthen our desire to "hope thou in God" (Psalm 42:11 KJV).

Bible Verses That Affirm Hope

Learn the following verses so that you can affirm them when your hope is running low:

And now faith, hope, and love abide, these three; and the greatest of these is love. (1 Corinthians 13:13)

What then are we to say about these things? If God is for [me], who is against [me]? (Romans 8:31)

I am confident of this, that the one who began a good work among you will bring it to completion by the day of Jesus Christ. (Philippians 1:6)

I can do all things through him who strengthens me. (Philippians 4:13)

We have this hope, a sure and steadfast anchor of the soul. (Hebrews 6:19)

I will never leave you or forsake you. (Hebrews 13:5)

Digging a Little Deeper

1. Read Psalm 118:24. What does this verse instruct us to do? Why is it important to rejoice in the gift of each new day and give thanks daily? How might reciting this verse before you get out of bed each morning help you to stay focused on the present rather than on the past or future?

2. How can we find happiness, even joy, in the midst of pain and loss? What makes this possible?

3. Read Exodus 16. What was God's purpose in providing manna one day at a time? When, in your own life, have you had to trust God day by day to provide provision or guidance?

4. What does it mean to live in "day-tight compartments"? Why do you think we have a problem doing this?

5. What is the meaning of the Greek word *entheos*? Read Colossians 1:27. How can knowing that Christ lives inside you help you to live with enthusiasm?

6. Respond to the following statement: *Enthusiasm is faith set on fire.*

7. Do you consider yourself enthusiastic? Why or why not? How might you practice living with enthusiasm?

8. How can we keep from giving in to discouragement and despair? What can help us to understand the power of hope?

9. In what ways does hope help us to grasp the future? Share an example from your life or the life of someone you know.

10. As Christians, what can we do to cultivate our hope?

11. Of the Bible verses on hope found on pages 44–45, which one means the most to you? Why?

CHAPTER FIVE

Choose to Have a Beautiful Tomorrow

Jesus Christ is the same yesterday and today and forever. (Hebrews 13:8)

I n a Dale Carnegie course, I learned this Carnegie quotation: "Today is the tomorrow that you worried about yesterday." This statement reminds us why we are often fragmented in our day-to-day living. We drag yesterday's problems into today while, at the same time, worrying about tomorrow.

We live in a world of constant change, and it seems to come at an ever-increasing pace. Yet despite all the change, we can know that we have a God who never changes—an unchanging God who loves us unconditionally.

"O Thou Who Changest Not, Abide With Me"

A number of years ago, while visiting my brother and his wife in North Carolina, I expressed a desire to drive to the town in which my brother and I had grown up. I wanted to see the house in which we had lived and which held so many memories for me. My brother warned me to be prepared for change, but I was stunned.

The entire neighborhood had been razed to make way for a new state highway that led to Interstate 40. The scene was surreal. I didn't recognize anything. I felt disoriented, as if we had never lived in that space.

Suddenly, the words of the Anglican pastor and hymn writer Henry F. Lyte flashed comfortingly into my mind: "Change and decay in all around I see; O thou who changest not, abide with me" (1847). Perhaps, as he wrote these words, he was thinking of Hebrews 13:8: "Jesus Christ is the same yesterday and today and forever." What a relief to remember that Jesus Christ, who revealed the nature of God to us, is the anchor that will always hold.

When our sons were ages eight and ten, our family took a vacation on a cruiser that belonged to my husband's brother. It was an interesting trip. When we went down the Tennessee River from Chattanooga, everything was perfect. The temperature was in the low 80s, and we often found good waters for fishing. At times, we docked at a marina to enjoy a restaurant meal. Sometimes the water was smooth and perfect for water skiing; other times, we would drop anchor and the four of us would go for a swim.

By the time we came to the Ohio River, however, we were surprised to find it at flood stage. We were dodging debris as large as trees—huge limbs and even animals. The water was so high that the locks through which we normally would go were now inundated, so we had to travel right over the top of them. Our destination was to anchor at Coney Island in Cincinnati so the boys could enjoy all the rides in the amusement park. There was no marina nearby, so we headed into the shore, tied the boat to a tree, and dropped anchor. We spent several pleasant hours in the park and returned to the boat.

In the middle of the night, my husband awakened to find our feet higher than our heads. The waters were receding, and we were quickly being beached. Heavy debris had gathered on the upriver side of the boat that had to be poled away before we could attempt to start the engines. The four of us worked and worked, finally freeing the boat; but when we started the engines, we found the anchor was caught in the debris and could not be retrieved. We lost the anchor, struck something underwater, and had to await daybreak before searching for a dry dock where a new propeller and rudder could be installed.

On the hazardous trip back to the Tennessee River, we had to dodge debris constantly. It was during this time that I gave thanks for the realization that, as Christians, we have an anchor that will hold against the storms and floods of life and that will help us when we are trapped. When our storms come, we need to remember that "Jesus Christ is the same yesterday and today and forever."

Authentic happiness comes when we have an anchor that holds no matter what the outward circumstances may be. For me, that anchor is Jesus Christ—Son of God, and Savior of all those who receive Him—who loves us unconditionally.

Accepting God's Unconditional Love

My twenty-six-year-old granddaughter, Ellen Mohney Gray, is a youth director in a large and active youth ministry in a local church. Last year, I asked her what she thought was the greatest problem her young people face. Perhaps I expected her to say drugs or alcohol or promiscuity, or even problems with their parents. Instead she said, "They don't know how much God really loves them."

As we talked about this, we concluded that many of the youth have never experienced unconditional love from their families or their peers.

Though parents may feel they're giving such love, young people often interpret it as "we love you if you are good" or "we love you if you make good grades" or "we love you if you do what we say." There is no security in the whole world like "we love you because you are you and because you belong to us." When young people have received unconditional love from parents or youth leaders, it is much easier to receive the incomparable love of God. Such love is like the present that has to be opened before it can be fully appreciated and enjoyed.

The Bible tells us that "God is love, and those who abide in love abide in God, and God abides in them" (1 John 4:16) and "This is my commandment, that you love one another as I have loved you" (John 15:12). The most powerful reminder of God's love for us is John 3:16, which says, "God so loved the world that he gave his only Son, so that everyone who believes in him may not perish but may have eternal life."

Believing these truths about God's love can transform how we see ourselves and thus change our life's direction. Yet this understanding usually comes through a person who, by living a more Christ-like life, shows us what is possible. Then, once we learn the truth about God's love, we know what it looks like when it is lived out. One picture is indeed better than a thousand words. All of us are called to be this kind of living example to others. As St. Francis reportedly said, "Preach the gospel to everyone and, if necessary, use words."

Unconditional Love Releases Us to Confidence and Joy

From my observation and experience over a number of years, I've concluded that if we are deeply loved, and if we recognize and receive that love, we have an unusual confidence and joy.

Let me introduce you to Marian. Because of a difficult childhood—desertion by her mother when Marian was eight and a controlling and abusive father—Marian always appeared shy, uncertain, and distrustful; all this despite the fact that she was unusually beautiful and extremely bright.

Many men wanted to date her, but her aura of "leave me alone, I don't trust anyone" made all of her relationships prickly—that is, until John came along. John, who was a few years older than Marian, had graduated from college and was established in his family's business. He grew up in a loving, Christian home and seemed to see Marian through different eyes. He saw her potential and had great compassion for anyone living in difficult circumstances.

I'm sure that Marian tried his patience in the beginning, as she struggled with fears of desertion and mistrust. Yet, gradually, like a swimmer learning to trust the water, Marian learned that she could count on what John said as truth. She blossomed! It was almost like seeing a caterpillar turn into a butterfly. Whereas she had been defensive and fearful, she became poised and confident and outgoing. She obviously saw herself through a different set of lenses. I marveled at the power of unconditional love on the human level.

I once heard an older, yet debonair and sophisticated, man say that he could always spot a woman who has been deeply loved because she exudes a kind of confidence. In the same way, I can find those Christians who are truly experiencing the unconditional love of God. They believe in themselves, in others, and in God. They don't take themselves too seriously. They usually have a great sense of humor. These people get along well with others and are not afraid to tackle big tasks. They reach out in love to even the most unloving.

Unconditional Love Can Turn a Life Around

The early life of Saul of Tarsus was as different from Marian's as night from day. Though living in a much earlier century, Saul's youth was pleasant and affirming. He was born into a home of privilege. His parents were Roman citizens—a huge advantage. It opened doors to travel, education, and to protection from Roman law. In addition, Saul was born into a devoutly Jewish home where Jewish law and practices were observed. He studied under the leading rabbis of his day and eventually became a member of the Sanhedrin, the highest governing body for Jews in that day.

When news of the growth of the new religious sect, called Followers of the Way, spread, Paul felt it necessary to take quick and decisive action against the group. He convinced the Sanhedrin of this necessity and volunteered for the job. Systematically, he ferreted out leaders of the Christian group and had them put to death, until God put a stop to it on the road to Damascus (Acts 9). Thereafter, it was said that the brilliant, visionary, and intense man experienced God's unconditional love through a powerful relationship with the risen Jesus.

Paul's life and our world were forever changed! He could later write, "I can do all things through him who strengthens me" (Philippians 4:13), and "If we live, we live to the Lord, and if we die, we die to the Lord; so then, whether we live or whether we die, we are the Lord's" (Romans 14:8). Paul encountered many difficulties, but because he had received God's unconditional love through Christ, he could write many of his inspiring and encouraging letters from prison, including the Letter to the Philippians, often called "The Epistle of Joy."

From Paul, Marian, and others, we learn lessons about unconditional love.

Lessons We Can Learn from Those Who Have Received God's Unconditional Love

In our national life, we learn from those who have gone before us so that, we hope, we do not have to make the same mistakes. Similarly, we can learn important lessons from other Christians, including current giants of faith. Let's consider some of these lessons.

Lesson 1: Our lives should not be defined by our past

All of us have done—or left undone—some things of which we are not proud. But if we drag the past into today and tomorrow, we are defined by it.

Though you probably have never committed murder, the apostle Paul had done so on numerous occasions; yet he received forgiveness from God. He received and internalized God's unconditional love and moved into a glorious—though not trouble-free—future. So can we!

Lesson 2: Our lives don't have to be defined by our circumstances

Marian's life had been defined by rejection and abuse until she received unconditional love from John, and through his love, she eventually was able to receive God's unconditional love. She then was no longer defined by her circumstances.

Paul never allowed himself to be defined by his difficulties—and he had plenty: shipwrecks, beatings, stonings, rejections, hunger, and imprisonments. Many of us would have given in to discouragement, despair, depression, self-pity, and anger. But Paul allowed God to define who he was and why he was alive—his reason for being.

Lesson 3: We must allow God to define us through Scripture

Created in the Image of God

Yet you have made [human beings] a little lower than God, and crowned them with glory and honor. (Psalm 8:5)

God created humankind in his image, in the image of God he created them; male and female he created them. (Genesis 1:27)

All of us have sinned and broken the image in which we were created, and thus fallen short of God's glory. (Romans 3:23, author's paraphrase)

Redeemed by Christ

God so loved the world that he gave his only Son, so that everyone who believes in him may not perish but may have eternal life. (John 3:16)

Empowered by the Holy Spirit

But to all who received him, who believed in his name, he gave power to become children of God. (John 1:12)

You will receive power when the Holy Spirit has come upon you. (Acts 1:8)

This is a powerful image and heritage! To claim it means to internalize it in our thoughts, expectations, and attitudes, and then to live it out in the nitty-gritty of everyday life.

Let me remind you that we are all Christians under construction. God hasn't finished with us yet. When I become discouraged with my progress and need more joy in my life, I remember Paul's words to the Philippians: "The one who began a good work among you will bring it to completion" (1:6). That is good news to us all!

Digging a Little Deeper

1. Read Hebrews 13:8. How can this verse help us during times of change and crisis?

2. What does it mean to say that Jesus Christ is the anchor that always holds?

3. Have you ever felt that the anchor has been cut away from your life and you are drifting away from shore—away from security and safety and everything familiar? Describe the situation. What finally happened?

4. Have there been changes and storms in your life during which you have forgotten that Christ is the anchor that always holds? In those times, who or what did you hope would keep you safe?

5. Respond to the following statement: *The greatest problem young people face today is that they do not know God loves them.* How can we help the youth of today come to know and to accept God's unconditional love? What would happen if more and more people—both young and old— were to accept God's unconditional love? What changes might we begin to see in our families, our schools, our workplaces, and our culture?

6. Read the following scripture verses: 1 John 4:16, John 15:12, and John 3:16. What do these verses tell us about God and God's love? What do they tell us about how God wants us to respond to this love? According to 1 John 4:16, what happens when we accept—abide in—God's love?

7. Why does the unconditional love of God release us to experience confidence and joy? Share an example from your own life or the life of someone you know to illustrate how this happens.

8. How does remembering that God loves us unconditionally enable us to love others in this way? Tell of a time when loving someone else unconditionally resulted in change—either in the individual, a situation, or both.

9. Read Acts 9. What in that Damascus road experience caused Paul's life to take a 180-degree turn? Have you had such an experience? If so, share as you are willing.

10. How does God's unconditional love enable us to endure trials, pain, and suffering? Share from your own life experience, if you are willing.

11. What defines your life right now? Is it the way God sees you—or something else? Read Psalm 8:5; Genesis 1:27; Romans 3:23; John 3:16; John 1:12; and Acts 1:8. What do these verses tell us about our identity and heritage as Christians?

12. Have you claimed this Christian identity and heritage, or are you defined by your past or present circumstances? How might your life be different this week if you were to truly celebrate the freedom and happiness you have in Christ?

CHAPTER SIX

Choose Laughter

A cheerful heart is a good medicine, but a downcast
spirit dries up the bones. (Proverbs 17:22)

She looked like an army drill sergeant—with a sturdy build, an abrupt speech, and a take-charge, no-nonsense manner. The airport waitress charged through the kitchen door and approached her customers with an "I need your order now" attitude.

One of her customers was a mild-mannered, distinguished-looking, gray-haired pastor who had been the featured speaker at a large gathering in the city the day before. He was taking an early morning flight back to his home. On that particular morning, he may have been sleepy or preoccupied with thoughts of his day's activities. At any rate, the burly waitress evidently perceived him as tense, even dour. As she descended upon his table, she said in a loud, gruff voice, "Lighten up, buttercup."

When the pastor told the story at a later gathering, we participants were convulsed with laughter. In the first place, the thought of this distinguished gentleman being called "buttercup" was so ridiculous that it was funny. Even more humorous was that he told the story on himself—

and with such witty description that we could practically see the sub-
stantial woman and almost smell the coffee she was pouring as she made
the impertinent remark.

As I reflected on that incident, I came to the conclusion that in a
world full of noise, pressure, and deadlines, we all would do well—particularly we Christians—to lighten up and laugh more. It was Mark Twain
who wrote, "Laughter is God's hand on the shoulder of a troubled world."

The Bible Encourages Laughter

In Proverbs 17:22, King Solomon gives us a reminder of why laughter
is so important: "A cheerful heart is a good medicine, but a downcast
spirit dries up the bones."

Sarah, wife of the biblical patriarch Abraham, must have had a merry
heart. I have often enjoyed the story of Sarah, who, when she was
advanced in years, doubled up with laughter upon being told that she and
Abraham were to have a baby. The miracle child who was born to them
was named Isaac, which means laughter. Although at first Sarah's laughter might have been out of doubt and disbelief, she later came to such
faith that she believed "for God all things are possible" (Matthew 19:26).
Then her laughter came from enjoyment of life, knowing that she wasn't
in charge of the universe. She could trust God for the future.

God must be more saddened than amused, however, when we, like
Sarah and Abraham, forget that we can accomplish unbelievable things
when we claim God's promises and seek to fulfill his purposes—or when
we forget our dependency upon him, strutting around with feelings of
imperial self-importance and self-sufficiency. Perhaps many of us need to
hear God say, "Lighten up, Buttercup"!

Solomon reminds us that even in laughter the heart may ache (Proverbs 14:13), but humor gives us a needed break from the pain of heartache. When we forget our dependence upon Christ or fail to remember what we can accomplish through his power, we need to lighten up and heed Paul's words: "I can do all things through [Christ] who strengthens me" (Philippians 4:13).

In his book *The Humor of Christ*, Elton Trueblood reminds us that Jesus said it is impossible for us to enter the kingdom of God unless we become as little children (Mark 10:15). Trueblood points out that a part of being childlike is playfulness and the ability to laugh and that even Christ had a sense of humor. Christ's humor often involves paradoxes—"Can a blind person guide a blind person? Will not both fall into a pit?" (Luke 6:39)—and exaggeration—"It is easier for a camel to go through the eye of a needle than for someone who is rich to enter the kingdom of God" (Mark 10:25).

Obviously, Jesus had a marvelous maturity. It included seriousness and laughter. Most of all, Jesus emphasized the joy of balanced living: "I have said these things to you so that my joy may be in you, and that your joy may be complete" (John 15:11). Joy is his gift to all his followers!

Laughter Is Good for Your Health

There is no doubt the Bible encourages laughter because God, who created us, knows that laughter is good for us. The healing power of laughter has been taught through the ages—from Aristotle to Kant to Locke. In recent years, however, the physical benefits of laughter have received increased attention. Many physical benefits of laughter have been studied and documented. Laughter can lower your blood pressure, heart rate, and stress level; improve nutritional benefits, breathing, and blood flow to the brain; restore your interest and energy; provide stimulation, strengthen the immune system, and help you fight disease.

Norman Cousins, who served as editor of *Saturday Review* for many years, laughed himself back to health and wrote about it in his book *The Anatomy of an Illness*. He witnessed firsthand the curative power of laughter as he dealt with his own life-threatening illness. Part of his rehabilitation routine was to rent old Laurel and Hardy movies and watch them for several hours each day. Not only was this a distraction from pain and a spirit-lifter but it also actually helped to strengthen his immune system. Later he was invited to join the staff of a medical school, where he helped patients understand the role of a positive attitude and laughter in their recovery.

As strange as it may seem, laughter can even help some people deal with grief. I have a friend whose husband was killed several years ago in an automobile accident. The couple had three children, and both parents were persons of steadfast Christian faith who practiced joy and laughter in their daily lives. As expected, the family went through a period of grief following the husband's sudden death.

My friend later told me that one day she realized they would never return to any form of normalcy unless they continued some of the fun activities they had enjoyed as a family—camping, biking, swimming in a lake near their home, and talking and singing around the campfire. At first, these activities were teary experiences, but they also were comforting. They provided opportunities for the children to talk about their dad, laugh about some of his eccentricities, and remember the values by which he had lived. "Continuing some of the fun activities we had enjoyed before Jim's death," my friend commented, "proved to be wonderfully healing."

Laughter Makes You a Happier Person

In addition to the many physical benefits of laughter, laughter also benefits your emotional stability and relationships. It is my observation that the people who laugh easily are those who are more understanding, more relaxed, more optimistic, and much more flexible. Simply put, laughter can help you to enjoy life more.

Those who laugh easily, who don't take themselves too seriously, and who look for the humor in life are not only healthier, happier people but also are more fun to be around! Laughter can actually bring you more friends, which, in turn, brings you more opportunities for experiencing joy.

Some Benefits of Laughter

1. Laughter helps us stay physically healthy and helps us to fight disease. Laughter is like internal aerobics. Our circulation and heart rate are improved; our blood pressure is lowered; our immune system is strengthened; and we are distracted from our pain.
2. Laughter improves our relationships.
3. Laughter restores our energy and interests and stimulates our creativity.
4. Laughter helps us enjoy life more.
5. Laughter relaxes us and lifts our spirits.
6. Laughter makes us more flexible and optimistic.
7. Laughter gives us a needed break from the pain of heartache.
8. Laughter helps us to deal constructively with problems and difficult situations.

Several years ago, I went to hear a well-known speaker. I had worked hard to clear my schedule and save enough time for the drive to the city where she was speaking. When I returned home, my husband asked eagerly, "Well, how did you like her? Did you enjoy the speech?"

Sadly, however, I had to admit that the whole experience was a downer. Although I agreed with everything she said, she was too intense! She never smiled or laughed or told a humorous incident. As a result, I was exhausted at the end of the hour. Granted, most of the other women present and I needed to confront some of the truths presented that day, but as the saying goes, "A little bit of sugar helps the medicine go down." A little bit of laughter that day would have made the truths easier to accept.

When you consider the many benefits of laughter, it may be one of the simplest and most effective ways to get "up" when you are feeling down. We may experience these benefits of laughter more fully by following four simple steps.

Four Simple Steps to Laughter

In his book *Maybe It's Time to Laugh Again*, Charles Swindoll writes that the three biggest joy killers are worry, stress, and fear. He says that although we can't control all the circumstances in our lives, we can, with the help of God, control our reactions. If we are a fearful, stressed-out worrier, we can learn to laugh again by following three simple steps—and I have added a fourth.

1. Look for humor in everyday life

Someone has said that if you can find something to laugh about early in the morning, you'll have a lighter touch throughout the day. I've discovered that many of my e-mails provide some good humor during days that are full of deadlines. Some of the humor is bland and even tasteless, but my friends usually screen it for me so that their e-mails always provide a chuckle. Recently, when I was not feeling very creative and definitely not "in the flow" for writing, I downloaded my unread e-mails from the night before. One story a friend had sent me was of an elderly couple named Esther and Mark who had grown up in the Great Depression. As a result, they were very reluctant to buy anything that wasn't absolutely necessary for survival—especially Esther.

Their big recreational event for the year was going to the county fair. Each year, Mark said, "I would like to go up for a ride in that airplane." Regretfully, Esther would say, "I know you want to experience some air travel, but the ride costs fifty dollars, and fifty dollars is fifty dollars."

After many years of the same conversation, Mark one day said, "Look, Esther, I am eighty-five years old. If I am ever going up in a plane, I need to do it now." Esther shook her head and said, "I know how badly you want that ride, but fifty dollars is fifty dollars." The pilot of the plane overheard their conversation and said that he would take them both up for fifty dollars, and if neither uttered a sound or said a word, they would get the ride absolutely free. Even Esther thought that was a good deal!

When they climbed aboard the antiquated plane with the open cockpit, they pledged to each other that they would be completely silent. The pilot went into his most daring routines—quick rollovers, rapid ascents, and more rapid dives. It was enough to make a seasoned flier queasy. This he did over and over again. There wasn't one sound from either of his two passengers. When they landed, the pilot turned to Mark and said, "I'll have to hand it to you. I was sure that there would be a scream from one of you, but not a peep." Mark replied, "Well, I almost yelled when Esther fell out, but fifty dollars is fifty dollars."

Of course, the story was pure fabrication. No one would let a mate fall out of a plane and not report it because of fifty dollars! Still, the ending was so unexpected that I laughed uproariously. The tension was broken, and I got back to business.

It's important to look for humor in everyday life.

2. When you feel yourself getting irritated or angry, count to ten and find something ludicrous in the situation

This step will help you deal with the situation more calmly, helping you to realize that whatever happened was not worth your getting upset. The American Football Conference playoff in 1987 between the Denver Broncos and the Cleveland Browns provides a good example.

It was near the end of the fourth quarter, and Cleveland had just scored. They were one touchdown ahead. Only one minute and fifty-seven seconds remained in the game. At the next kickoff, Denver fumbled the ball on its one-yard line. The commentators assumed that the game was over. Denver fans groaned and mourned the loss; hostile Cleveland fans threw dog biscuits on the field. Even the announcers were speculating who Cleveland would play in the Super Bowl. Time out was called, and John Elway and the Denver Broncos went into a huddle in their own end zone. In that chance, seemingly hopeless situation, Keith Bishop, the all-American left tackle, said with a twinkle in his eyes, "Hey, guys, now we have got 'em just where we want 'em." It was such a ludicrous statement that the whole team burst out laughing. One player laughed so much he fell on the ground. In that moment, laughter relieved anxiety and tension and infused the team with calm confidence.

What followed has become known in football annals as "The Drive." The Denver Broncos regained the ball, drove down the field, and scored in the last seconds of the game. They won the game in overtime and went to the 1988 Super Bowl.

This is a great example of how humor can relieve stress and tension. Keith Bishop must have counted to ten or taken a deep breath in order not to react in panic or anger. Then he was able to find something humorous in the situation.

It has been said that laughter is our best weapon and the one least used. It is true. How many of us regularly use humor to relieve tension and help us deal with problems?

3. Remember that some of our concerns are "much ado about nothing"

Every concern we have seems important at the time, but the truth is that the outcome of many of our concerns will make no difference in ten years. Though we must seek to right the wrongs, the weight of the world is not on our shoulders. God is still in control, so we can laugh and love and trust God for the future.

Early one morning, I was hard at work in my office at the church when suddenly the door flew open and in walked a young woman, sobbing uncontrollably. Sally was one of the most active young adults in our church. She was attractive and intelligent, she had a good job, and she had just celebrated her first wedding anniversary.

Judging from her sobs, I thought she and Tim must have had a serious relationship problem, or that someone close to her had died. Finally, when she was able to stop crying and talk, she said that she and Tim had not been included on the guest list of a big party given by the supervisor in Tim's company. "This must mean that Tim isn't doing well," she said, "because everybody else in his department is invited. Also, we had this couple to dinner just a month ago, and now they have snubbed us. It's just not fair!"

It seemed to me that she had blown the whole thing out of proportion, but I knew that Sally was feeling the pain of rejection; so I let her talk through her feelings. Then I asked, "Are you sure that you and Tim are the only couple who were excluded?" No, she wasn't. In fact, she knew of only two in the department who were invited.

"Then this had nothing to do with Tim's competence at work," I suggested. "And haven't there been times when you couldn't invite everyone you would have liked to have at a party?" I asked. Nodding, she said, "Of course. But we had that couple for dinner just last month." Suddenly she grinned and said, "Guess I am just dealing with hurt pride."

I smiled and reminded her that the pain of rejection can be very real, and that all of us have to face it from time to time. By then she was able to look at things more objectively. She straightened her shoulders, dried her tears, and headed for another appointment, calling to me, "Thanks for helping me see that this was not the end of the world."

As she left, I thought of how often we spend hours worrying and crying over things that won't matter at all in a few days or weeks or years. Incidentally, Tim later became president of that company!

When we get away from a situation in order to see it in clearer perspective, we can relax and even laugh at ourselves.

4. Learn to laugh at yourself

We receive a subtle benefit from the ability to laugh at ourselves; it helps us to see ourselves in proper perspective—to realize that no matter what our credentials, we are not the center of the universe.

About ten years ago, I was speaking at a Sunday through Wednesday Lenten event in a large, active church in Cleveland, Ohio. It was the afternoon of the last day. In my hotel room, I put on the green wool dress I would be wearing that evening. Since I had brought a pair of black shoes and a pair of brown shoes for the week, I tried one of each color to see which I liked best with the dress.

Before I could check them out in the full-length mirror, the telephone rang. It was a church member who wanted to talk with me about a serious marital problem she was facing. We talked for thirty minutes or more before the call was interrupted by the hotel operator. She said that the associate minister was in the lobby to take me to my dinner appointment. Forgetting all about my two different-colored shoes, I grabbed my coat and went to the lobby.

That evening I stood before the congregation for the service and later stood in line for a reception in my honor—all in my mismatched shoes. It was not until I was back in my hotel room, talking by telephone to my husband, that I noticed my mistake. We both had a great laugh.

A postscript to that experience is that last summer I was speaking at Lake Side Assembly on Lake Erie. In the audience was a woman who had been in my Cleveland audience when the incident had occurred. When we talked later, I asked if she had noticed the mismatched shoes. "Oh, yes, we all did, but we thought it was a new southern style," she said. We might as well learn to laugh at ourselves because we *will* make mistakes!

On another occasion, I was speaking to a very large group of very conservative Christians. At one point in my speech, I meant to say, "I live in an all-male family—one husband and two sons." Instead I said, "Two husbands and one son." There was an audible gasp in the audience. Intuitively, I knew better than to ignore it. I stopped and asked, "What did I say?" One man called out, "That you are a bigamist." It was my turn to gasp, "Oh, my goodness. No! I have a hard enough time with one." The auditorium exploded with laughter and applause, and the tension evaporated with humor.

Mark Twain was right: "Laughter is the hand of God on a troubled world." Laughter makes us healthier, improves our relationships, restores our energy, stimulates our creativity, lifts our spirits, and enables us to deal more constructively with problems. No wonder the Bible encourages laughter!

Digging a Little Deeper

1. Read again Proverbs 17:22. In what ways does a merry heart do good like medicine? When have you experienced this truth in your own life?

2. What does Proverbs 14:13 tell us? Given the truth of these words, how can humor be helpful during times of heartache?

3. Read John 15:11. Jesus, at the time he was facing the cross, gave the disciples these words as his last will and testament. How does Jesus' joy sustain us as we experience gloom and discouragement?

4. Think of someone who looks for humor in life and is fun to be around. How does being around such a person affect you?

5. Do you agree that people who laugh easily tend to be more understanding, relaxed, optimistic, and flexible? Why or why not?

6. Read and discuss the benefits of laughter listed on page 61. Which benefit are you most in need of at this time, and why?

7. Why is it important to look for humor in everyday life? What are some ways we can be intentional about looking for humor each day?

8. Why do people who worry unnecessarily find it hard to see humor in life?

9. No matter what our credentials or how important our position, why is it important for us to laugh at ourselves and not take ourselves too seriously? If you are willing, share a story of a time when tension was relieved with humor.

10. Even Job in the midst of his troubles was told, "[God] will yet fill your mouth with laughter, and your lips with shouts of joy" (Job 8:21). Do you believe this? Why or why not?

CHAPTER SEVEN

Choose Fitness of Body, Mind, and Spirit

Come to me, all you that are weary and are carrying

heavy burdens, and I will give you rest. (Matthew 11:28)

Y ou don't have to stay the way you are." This sentence, which was written on the chalkboard of a religion class I took in college, changed my life. I had come into the classroom feeling burdened. The letter I held in my hands was from my mother, telling me of problems at home. In addition, I was into my usual pattern of negative thinking—"I'm too fat" (I had gained only three pounds over the Christmas break and was well within my ideal weight); "I'm not smart enough" (I had made a B+ on an ancient history exam, so I felt like a failure); "I'll never be a real leader" (I had just been elected president of our student Christian organization, one of the three major offices on campus). I had a way of focusing on problems rather than on possibilities.

That day in class, the professor reminded us that Jesus said, "I came that they may have life, and have it abundantly" (John 10:10). He also told us that the Bible outlined the proper care of our bodies, our thought processes, and our spirits. Then he emphasized what he had written on the board: "You don't have to stay the way you are." He told us that through Christ we could become more than conquerors. As Paul said to the Romans, "In all these things [body, mind, and spirit] we are more than conquerors through him who loved us" (Romans 8:37). Suddenly I realized that, although Christ had redeemed me when I committed my life to him, he expected me to cooperate with him in my growth toward wholeness. It was an ah-ha moment that still enables me to live in excitement about the future.

In this chapter, we will discover that personal happiness involves growth in our understanding of physical, mental, and spiritual fitness. Let's first look at our physical bodies.

Caring for Your Body

I love the story about the three bricklayers who were working daily on a new building. One day while the men were taking their lunch break, a visitor passed by the men, who were seated in different places. He asked each of the three men the same question: "What are you doing?" The first man, who was working strictly to earn a pay check, replied, "I'm working for $9.00 an hour." When the visitor asked the same question of the second man, he replied, "I'm laying bricks." The third worker fairly beamed when he answered, "I'm building a cathedral."

In his first letter to the members of the church in Corinth, Paul reminds us, "Do you not know that your body is a temple of the Holy Spirit within you, which you have from God, and that you are not your own? For you were bought with a price; therefore glorify God in your body" (1 Corinthians 6:19-20).

The psalmist tells us a similar truth when he declares, "I praise you, for I am fearfully and wonderfully made" (Psalm 139:14). Yet, instead of treating our bodies like the magnificent works of art they are, we often treat them like old clunkers. We don't give our bodies high-performance fuel or protect them from the elements. We give them only minimal care but expect them to perform at top speed. We push them beyond their limits, and we are surprised that they have to spend so much time in the repair shop.

Several years ago, the American Dairy Association used a catchy little song for their TV marketing campaign. The opening line was "There's a new you coming every day." This slogan was based on the theory that new cells are born in our bodies every day and that over a period of seven years we get a whole new body—except for the enamel on our teeth. I don't know about you, but I hope I get a better-looking body the next time around!

Obviously, our sense of well-being and happiness is enhanced when we see our bodies as temples of the living God and give them the care and feeding they deserve. While happiness is not solely dependent on good health, a healthy, energetic body allows our witness to be stronger and God to be glorified. The truth is that we are less stressed and happier when we eat nutritionally and exercise regularly.

Consider the following proven ways to take good care of your body and improve your physical health:

1. Plan a suitable exercise program, and then work your plan

Physical therapists say we need three types of exercise: aerobic exercise, stretching, and calisthenics or weight-bearing exercise. Aerobic exercises such as walking, jogging, biking, cross-country skiing, and swimming develop cardiovascular efficiency—which is the ability of the heart to pump blood through your body—and increase endurance. Stretching warms and loosens your muscles and helps dissipate lactic acid so that you won't feel as sore and stiff. Stretching exercises are good to do when you first awaken and get out of bed, as well as throughout the day. Simple calisthenics or exercising with weights increases strength and helps prevent bones from becoming brittle and fragile. It doesn't take a lot of weight for this to be effective. Three- to five-pound weights are adequate for most people.

The temptation for all of us is to say, "I don't have time to exercise." Actually, exercise is so important that we don't have time *not* to exercise! Achieving a longer, healthier, less stressful life is motivation enough to set aside a minimum of thirty minutes three days a week for exercise. If you can exercise for one hour rather than thirty minutes, or for five days a week rather than three, you'll benefit even more. Remember that one of the very best exercises of all is simply to walk thirty minutes a day.

2. Eat nutritionally

Nutritionists tell us that what we eat drastically affects the way we feel about ourselves. Diet affects not only our weight but also our energy level, our mood swings, and our ability to throw off disease.

Determine to eat foods that are high in fiber and low in fat, sodium, and sugar. Examples are whole grain breads and cereals, brown rice, green leafy vegetables, legumes, and fruit. Of course, there are countless resources on the subject of nutrition. At times when I have had to lose a few pounds, I have felt the unwritten rule is "if it tastes good, spit it out." Actually, that is not true. The rules are: Make wise food choices, eat smaller portions, and practice self-control.

In addition to making wise food choices, keep an eye on your caloric intake. Remember that after thirty-five years of age, our metabolism decreases and we need to lower our caloric intake. A good goal is to stay within five pounds of your ideal weight (ask your doctor for a chart providing this information).

3. Get sufficient rest and sleep

Doctors tell us that if we want to keep our minds sharp, we need to get seven to eight hours of sleep each night. A nutritionist who was teaching at a seminar in a local hospital said that if we get inadequate sleep, we can gain weight. The reason, of course, is that when we are tired, we tend to snack on high-calorie food.

There are other dangers to getting insufficient rest. A good friend was driving his family from Illinois to Atlanta to check out Candler School of Theology at Emory University, where he hoped to enroll in the fall. It was early in the evening, and other members of the family were napping in the car. He dozed off to sleep, hit a bridge abutment, and his parents and younger brother and sister were killed. The young man lived, but he was seriously injured and his life has never been the same. Adequate rest may be a matter of life and death.

4. Have a physical examination annually

Diseases can develop quickly, and an annual physical is absolutely necessary. My mother was a procrastinator when it came to visiting her doctor. My brother, sister, and I are convinced that the cancer that took her life could have been caught at an earlier stage and treated if she had had regular checkups. One of the best preventive medicines, I believe, is an annual physical examination.

5. Establish a few close relationships (both family and non-family members) that are characterized by acceptance and trust

In his book *Future Shock*, Alvin Toffler calls these relationships "stability zones." We must plan for time and energy to develop these relationships.

In all the books I have read on happiness, one overriding theme is that the happiest people are the ones who have strong inter-personal relationships with family and close friends. God didn't create us to be lonely, alienated human beings. We are born into families, and we need to nurture these and other important relationships in our lives. This involves showing respect for one another, being willing to communicate, caring, making a commitment of time and energy, and being there for one another—attending events in which loved ones participate and being there in good times and bad. The Bible calls this "bear[ing] . . . one another's burdens, and so fulfill[ing] the law of Christ" (Galatians 6:2 KJV).

6. Develop a career or avocation that is fulfilling

One of the good things today is that you may have four or five careers in your lifetime. Twenty-five years ago, people usually went to work for one company and stayed until they retired. Most people today believe they are not only making a living but also making a life. I believe that where our talents meet the needs of the world, that's where we are called to be. This means we need to know what our gifts and talents are and what we truly enjoy doing. There may be times when, for financial reasons, we need to take a job we don't particularly like; but at the same time, we can find an avocation (a volunteer job) in which we can share with joy and enthusiasm.

7. Try new experiences that will add freshness to life

Do you always drive to work or church or the movies along the same route? Begin to change this habit. Do you have friends in your age group only? Begin to cultivate friends who are younger and older than you. This is especially possible through jobs that are inter-generational. Several years ago, I began to teach a class of single adults, which enabled me to see the world in clearer perspective. We need to get out of our comfort zones because, eventually, they become ruts. Remember that you don't grow old; you get old because you don't grow!

8. Exercise control over the number of stressors you are experiencing at any given time

Though there are some stressors in life that we cannot control, such as illness and death and the behaviors of others, there are other stressors that we can choose to avoid or delay when our stress level is already high. For example, if you are going through a divorce or grieving the death of a loved one, it's probably not the best time to voluntarily take on a job change or move to a new location or have a confrontation that will end a friendship.

Even high stressors such as getting married, having a baby, going on vacation, and hosting a family reunion can be just one more thing that pushes you over the top. Keep a balance in life by saying "no" to some things, taking time for yourself, renewing your spirit, and developing a calm, inner life. All of these things enable us to live with more balance and joy.

9. Learn to delegate and say no without feeling guilty

One of the best ways to alleviate stress is to delegate. If you are a parent, teach children to take over household responsibilities as soon as possible.

If you are in the workforce, learn to delegate some of your responsibilities. Learning to say no is likewise important—particularly for persons who have low self-esteem or who have a strong need to please others. Saying no involves establishing priorities and setting goals.

Being organized, however, does not mean being rigid. There are times when you have to put priorities aside for something of greater importance. For example, there are times when your spouse, your children, or your boss may need your time and attention right away, and you need to respond. That's being flexible, but it is not the kind of flexibility seen in a reed that bends before every wind that blows. Rather, you have decided to change your priorities.

My formula for saying "no" is (1) establish priorities—they may change from year to year because of children's ages or job requirements; (2) serve somewhere for Christ and his church; (3) keep family relationships strong; and (4) work, play, and pray. Learn to say "no" to things that keep you from fulfilling your priorities. Remember that it is in prayer time that we are helped to determine true priorities.

10. Don't procrastinate; meet your problems head on

Dreading a situation can cause more stress than dealing with a problem. Procrastination is difficult to overcome because we rationalize that we are just postponing taking action rather than deciding not to take action. Yet, sadly, the grand thief of procrastination robs us of time, motivation, decisiveness, and strong personal relationships. Let's recognize this thief and take steps to prevent it from breaking and entering and destroying our lives.

Three practices have helped me hold the thief at bay. First, every New Year's Eve, I write down ten great expectations for the coming year in four areas: physical, mental, spiritual, and relational. Then I go over them regularly in my mind and make an action plan for each one. Second, each evening before going to sleep, I list the six most important things I want to accomplish the next day, excluding ordinary chores such as dishwashing, making beds, and so forth. And third, my quiet time each morning "sets my sails" for the day. This is a time when I read scripture and other inspirational material and seek God's guidance and creative ideas in prayer.

11. Make a list of all the things that bother you, and write beside each what action you will take

Let's say, for example, that I am concerned about my husband's health. He has had some heart problems, and I realize that he's putting on weight and not exercising. My action plan would not include nagging but would include serving fewer breads and desserts and suggesting that the two of us take walks each evening. As he builds up his stamina through walking, he'll be able to take on more strenuous exercise.

If you can't do anything to change your situation, such as a job, you still have three choices: accept it, continue to be frustrated and angry, or leave the situation. Remember the prayer attributed to Reinhold Niebuhr: "God, grant me the serenity to accept the things I cannot change, the courage to change the things I can, and the wisdom to know the difference."

12. Practice meditation and prayer daily

Meditation and prayer are perhaps the two most successful methods of handling stress. Quiet meditation and prayer can slow your heart and respiratory rates, lower your blood pressure, clear your thinking, relieve anxiety, and help you sleep better. Isaiah, a wise man and prophet of God, knew this thousands of years ago. He wrote:

> Those who wait for the LORD shall renew their strength,
>   they shall mount up with wings like eagles,
> they shall run and not be weary,
>   they shall walk and not faint. (Isaiah 40:31)

The kind of meditation I'm talking about is different from other forms of meditation in which individuals rid their minds of all thoughts and then think whatever thoughts come to them. In Christian meditation, the individual focuses on God's Word (for example, Psalms 1 and 2) so that he or she may understand and better follow Christ.

Prayer, on the other hand, is our conversation with God in which we give him praise and thanksgiving, make our petitions known, and listen for his guidance.

13. Take mini-vacations and laugh more often

When things are fast and furious at home or work, take a few minutes for a mini-vacation. Close your eyes and relax your body. Now, in your imagination go to a spot that is very peaceful to you. Soon your mind will be calm and your stress level will be lower. Remember that ships don't come in on rough waters. You need to become calm in order to think clearly.

One of the things that bothers me is that many of us Christians are so task-oriented that we don't seem to be enjoying life. I still struggle with this problem at times, although I am somewhat better than I used to be. In my case, this problem developed because I was a perfectionist. My focus was on doing everything well for God instead of internalizing God's love and enjoying God's world.

There is so much to bring us joy and laughter in life, but we can't see it if we are driven toward perfectionism. Learning the art of relaxation is a vital skill in this procedure. Likewise, training yourself to see humor all around you will enable you not only to enjoy life more but also to be a healthier person.

14. Learn and practice sound financial management

Many people are robbed of inner peace because they worry over finances. In this consumer-driven culture where millions of people are maxed out on their credit cards, one of our greatest needs is to learn good financial management. Many churches hold financial management classes, as do community colleges and other community organizations such as the Chamber of Commerce. One thing is certain: we will never have peace or happiness if we are worrying about unpaid bills or foreclosures on our homes. One of the best first steps we can take is to cut up all of our credit cards.

15. Strive to keep a healthy balance in your life— physically, mentally, emotionally, socially, and spiritually

One of the needs most often expressed in my seminars on life management is the need for balance in our personal lives as we strive to juggle career and family. I have found it to be a lifelong struggle, although it is more intense while the children are still living at home.

I believe the answer involves organizing our lives around five priorities: (1) our relationship to God through Christ; (2) our relationship with our family; (3) our career and personal growth—giving both creative thought and planning; (4) our friendships; and (5) our service to our community. You can't have every week of your life balanced precisely; but if your overall life is in balance, you can find happiness.

Renewing Your Mind

The biggest battle I have ever fought has been with my thoughts. In fact, it took me years to understand how "alive" thoughts really are.

In my young adult years, I expected the worst in every situation. This pattern came from habitually thinking negative and discouraging thoughts. My change from negative thoughts to thoughts of peace, confidence, and trust in Christ began when I read *A Guide to Confident Living* by Dr. Norman Vincent Peale. As the author told of his own battle with negativity and inferiority, I saw what my thought pattern was doing to me and realized that I had the power to choose my thoughts.

> I appeal to you therefore, brothers and sisters, by the mercies of God, to present your bodies as a living sacrifice, holy and acceptable to God, which is your spiritual worship. (Romans 12:1)

> Do not be conformed to this world, but be transformed by the renewing of your minds, so that you may discern what is the will of God. (Romans 12:2)

Very slowly, but oh so gratefully, I began to turn from negativism, confusion, anger, and resentment to trust, peace, and positive hope. Though the process didn't happen overnight, it was worth all the effort and prayer I invested in it. There is no way in the world I would return to that troubled period. I can sincerely pray the prayer that Gertrude Behanna, a well-known Christian speaker, would always pray as she closed her seminars—the prayer of a long-deceased slave: "O Lord, I ain't what I wanta be. O Lord, I ain't what I oughta be. And O Lord, I ain't what I'm gonna be. But thanks, Lord, I ain't what I used to be!" Remember that you have the power to choose your thoughts, so choose to be transformed in your thinking by the renewing of your mind.

One of the best ways we can renew our minds is through Bible study. Recently, I joined a small group in my church to study the Beatitudes and Christ's Sermon on the Mount. I especially enjoyed studying the seventh beatitude: "Blessed are the peacemakers."

One of the Christian attributes I have always sought is the peace that passes understanding (Philippians 4:6-7); yet as a wife and mother, I have often allowed little, inadvertent things to affect me and thus upset our entire family. I am sure that my husband, Ralph, believed the saying, "If Mamma ain't happy, ain't nobody happy"!

As recently as last night, I allowed something a friend said to destroy temporarily my sense of calm and peace. Feeling as if I were in the midst of a civil war, I remembered this poem by Edward Sanford Martin:

> Within my earthly temple there's a crowd.
> There's one of us that's humble, one that's proud.
> There's one who's broken-hearted for his sins;
> And one who, unrepentant, sits and grins.
> There's one who loves his neighbor as himself,
> And one who cares for naught but fame and pelf.
> From much corroding care I should be free,
> If once I could determine which one is me.
> ("My Name Is Legion," in *Masterpieces of Religious Verse*, ed. James
> Dalton Morrison [New York: Harper and Bros., 1948], 274.)

As I thought about this, I realized that the thoughts I feed and care for and renew will determine who I am.

Our growth toward wholeness requires that we regularly renew our minds. One of the ways I do this is by practicing a daily quiet time.

Practicing a Daily Quiet Time

Time alone with God each day helps me renew my mind. My daily quiet time is the time when I leave the hustle and bustle of the world and move into the eternal dimension of life. For that thirty- to forty-minute period, I feel as if I have one foot in heaven. This is the practice I use:

1. Center yourself in God's presence

Go physically to the place where you have your daily quiet time. (If going there physically is impossible, go there in your mind.) Allow yourself to become totally centered in God's presence. Begin to breathe deeply and then to grow calm. I often recite or meditate on these words from the hymn "Dear Lord and Father of Mankind":

> Drop thy still dews of quietness
> Till all our strivings cease,
> Take from our souls the strain and stress
> And let our ordered lives confess
> The beauty of thy peace.
> (John Greenleaf Whittier, 1872)

2. Cast all your cares on God

First Peter 5:7 tells us, "Cast all your anxiety on him, because he cares for you." Release all your anxieties, worries, and concerns. This is a time of body and mind relaxation. I breathe in the Holy Spirit and breathe out my fears, worries, and anxieties. The more relaxed I become, the more I turn loose of my problems, listing them by name. This simple exercise is a powerful reminder of the words of the hymn "Take your burdens to the Lord and leave them there."

3. Count your blessings

In the quietness, begin to count all of your blessings. Remember and give thanks for the ways in which God has blessed you in the past. Recall that God has promised a way out even when you don't see one.

In a consumer-oriented culture, it is so easy to think of all we don't have. The simple act of gratitude opens our hearts to God's goodness.

Remember the old hymn that says, "Count your many blessings, name them one by one, and it will surprise you what the Lord has done."

4. Grab hold of a creative solution, or let go of whatever is bothering you

I have learned that in the quietness, I either receive an idea for a creative solution or I am able to let go of whatever has been disturbing me. In Acts 28:1-6 is the wonderful story of Paul at Malta. Paul, along with a number of other prisoners, was en route to meet the Emperor when the ship ran aground on the island of Malta. The natives began to build a fire to warm their guests. When Paul picked up some brush to add to the fire, a serpent, driven out by the heat, latched onto his hand. The natives, confident that he would begin to swell and then die, were amazed that Paul simply shook off the snake and remained perfectly well. Sometimes we simply need to shake off the frustrations and irritants that derail our thinking.

5. Offer praise

If possible, I like to close the session by listening to hymns or praise music, or by simply giving thanks to God. We will never be able to escape all the irritants of life and the temptation to react negatively, but we can choose to "be still, and know that I am God" (Psalm 46:10), which naturally leads to praise.

There is power in praise to transform our thoughts, attitudes, and actions. For me, reading psalms and singing praise songs transports me into the presence of the Holy One.

Cultivating a Quiet Inner Life

I have discovered that it is important to renew my mind not only by having a daily quiet time, but also by developing a quiet inner life. In his poem "The Place of Peace," Edwin Markham wrote:

At the heart of the cyclone tearing the sky,
And flinging the clouds and the towers by,
    Is a place of central calm.
(from *The Shoes of Happiness and Other Poems* [Garden City, N.Y.:
Doubleday], 1915)

Whether we are watching the news on television, reading a newspaper, or actually being a participant in a high-tech, fast-moving world, we are surrounded by a world full of noise, violence, and conflicts. Though it is not easy, developing a quiet inner life is a necessity if we are to keep the peace that Jesus promised.

When we have a quiet inner life, our very dispositions bless others. In his first letter to the Thessalonians, the apostle Paul writes: "This should be your ambition: to live a quiet life, minding your own business . . . , just as we told you before. As a result, people who are not Christians will trust and respect you, and you will not need to depend on others for enough money to pay your bills" (4:11-12 TLB).

I have a friend who has such a quiet dignity and inner joy that people delight in having her as a guest. She is an author and speaker and serves on several prestigious boards. Yet there is not a pretentious bone in her body. I've seen her in groups where there are great theological differences and in other groups where political opinions are diverse. She never pushes her beliefs, but when asked, she speaks with convincing clarity—and never patronizingly. As a result, people listen with respect when she speaks. She blesses others through her calm, inner life.

I believe we cultivate a quiet inner life by knowing who we are in Christ—created in the image of God, redeemed by Jesus Christ, and empowered by the Holy Spirit. Also, we need to practice calmness. Instead of just reacting to a situation, we need to calm our spirits and look at the situation objectively. In the depths of the cool calmness, I believe we are given intuitive sensitivities to what others are thinking and feeling. It is a much easier way to negotiate than loud confrontation.

Allowing the Holy Spirit to Guide and Direct Your Life

All we have studied in this chapter indicates that the outer you houses the real you, the eternal you, which is your mind and spirit. These separate portions of our beings—body, mind, and spirit—need to be blended together to reflect who we are: faithful disciples of Jesus Christ. Actually, it is the spirit that houses God's gift of the Holy Spirit—the spirit of Christ—who guides, directs, and empowers us.

In the last church we served during Ralph's active ministry, one of my favorite members was Ruth Huffaker Beard. Ruth and her family were loyal church members and people of spiritual depth. Yet it was only recently, when members were asked to tell something of their spiritual journeys for a book the church was publishing, that I learned the power of the Holy Spirit in Ruth's life. In the book she recounted the following experience, and before her recent death, she gave me permission to share it here:

> At age seventeen, I was a high school senior and a debater. The Forensic League sponsored a tournament at a nearby college over a weekend in 1941. Our debate and oratory coach took my team and another to represent our high school.
>
> As the first debate started, I collapsed—completely paralyzed with eyes closed. I could hear the students discussing my condition, but I couldn't move. When the ambulance came, the crew called me by name and said that since it was so cold outside they would put the sheet over my face until we reached the warm ambulance. On the way out of the building, I

heard several students speculating, "She's already dead; they've covered her head." (Remember that the hearing is the last sense to go!)

By the time we reached the hospital in Abingdon, Virginia, I was completely unconscious. Six doctors were trying to diagnose my situation. After a few tests, they decided that it was cerebral hemorrhage at the base of the brain. Medical reports later noted that I had two spinal punctures to relieve pressure on the brain. During one of these procedures I had an out-of-body experience. I was against the ceiling on the opposite side of the room, looking down at my own body. I was cold and in a fetal position with a doctor at my back. The nurse was on the other side of the table with her back to the wall and her hand on my neck. I felt no pain, no anxiety; I was just a detached spectator.

Much later when I could talk I discussed this with the nurse. She asked how I could possibly describe the scene. "You were unconscious when you went down and unconscious when you returned to your bed. Your eyes have been closed ever since you entered the hospital," she said.

Two weeks later when I regained consciousness, my right side was completely paralyzed, my tongue was numb, and my right eye was out of focus. I was silently repeating scripture to myself. I kept asking God why the traumatic event had happened to me. I knew that I had irretrievably lost ten years of piano instruction. That was a devastating realization, for I had hoped to use my music background in my career in Christian education. I was really angry with God for this tragic turn in my life. No matter how many questions I asked, God was very gentle with me.

Since I couldn't talk, I was unable to verbalize my reflections. As I continued my silent debate with myself, I became aware that another entity was talking with me. The Holy Spirit was guiding my thoughts and answering my questions!

Since this experience I have never felt alone. For the last three years I have had multiple mycelia (cancer of the brain marrow). During this time I have not been depressed, nor am I afraid of death. I know without a doubt that our heavenly father walks in the way with me. In my darkest hours, in the deepest holes, the Holy Spirit is always with me.

As I read Ruth Beard's story, it reminded me of something I already knew: When we commit our lives to Christ, we will never walk alone. The Holy Spirit will be given to live within us.

In her book *Something More*, the late Katherine Marshall tells how the Holy Spirit leads, guides, comforts, and empowers us. The Holy Spirit is given us at baptism, but only when we open every room of our lives—even the attic of our memories—to the Spirit's presence are we filled with the Spirit. We can quench the Spirit through disobedience and doubt.

What an awesome God we serve! If we allow it, the Holy Spirit will be at work in our entire being—body, mind, and spirit—to make us all God intends us to be.

Digging a Little Deeper

1. In 1 Corinthians 6:19, the apostle Paul reminds members of the church at Corinth that their bodies are the temple of the Holy Spirit. What are some of the cultural evidences that, as a society, we do not treat our bodies as temples? If you were to live daily in the full awareness that your body is a temple of the Holy Spirit, what changes would you need to make in the way you care for and treat your body?

2. Read Psalm 139:14. What does this verse tell us about our bodies? In light of what God's Word says, why do you think so many Christians treat their bodies as old clunkers rather than the wonderful, magnificent works of art they are?

3. Do you agree that a healthy, energetic body allows us to have a stronger witness, giving greater glory to God? Why or why not?

4. What are the three types of exercise we should do at least three times a week? Which is hardest for you, and why? What would help you to

be more intentional and disciplined about exercising regularly? Share ideas and encouragement with one another.

5. What is one wise choice you need to make to keep your body, the temple of God, in good condition?

6. Read Isaiah 40:31. How can following the advice of the prophet Isaiah help us to manage stress? What does it mean to wait on the Lord? What are some other ways we can manage stress?

7. What in your vocation gives you such a sense of fulfillment or adventure that you know where God intends you to be?

8. What is one reason that adequate sleep and rest are important?

9. What area of your life is keeping you out of balance? What will you do to correct it?

10. Read Romans 12:1-2. What do these verses instruct us to do? Why are we to renew our minds, and what is the result?

11. Though we have the power to choose our thoughts and transform our thinking, why do you think so many Christians feel trapped in negative and anxious thought patterns? Share some practical examples of times and ways we can exercise our power to choose our thoughts and thinking patterns.

12. What is the hardest thing for you when it comes to keeping a daily quiet time?

13. Read 1 Thessalonians 4:7-12. What does the apostle Paul say is the result of living a quiet life? How can cultivating a quiet *inner* life contribute to this? What are some ways we can develop a quiet inner life?

14. Does your life lack spiritual power? Have you invited the Holy Spirit into every room of your life? If not, why not?

CHAPTER EIGHT

Choose Prayer Power

He was praying in a certain place, and after he had fin-
ished, one of his disciples said to him, "Lord, teach us to pray,
as John taught his disciples." (Luke 11:1)

I was only seven years old and in the second grade when I became terrified of praying. My Sunday school teacher, Miss Jones, was a tall,
"proper" lady who had volunteered to teach in what was then called
the primary department. Though I am sure she was a devout Christian,
she must not have had any training in childhood education. She also had
no love for a room full of wiggly seven-year-olds.

That must be why she decided to control us by fear. She told us that
God was a very big man who wore a long, black robe. He sat behind a big,
black desk on which there was a big, black book. Within that black book
was the name of each of us. When we did something wrong, or even
thought something wrong, God put a big, black mark by our names.
When we had a certain number of black marks, he marked our names off
completely. I was sure that meant certain death, or at least going to hell
when my life ended. Every Sunday, I dreaded going to Sunday school, and

every Sunday, I walked out of my class terrified that my name would be marked off in God's big, black book.

My mother heard my prayers at night, and I was still saying the "Now I lay me down to sleep" prayer. When I got to the "If I should die before I wake" part, I would mumble something else. Finally, I got to the place that when my mother came to my room, I told her I had already said my prayers. Soon, she began to connect my behavior at prayer time with my nightmares. It took her several weeks of probing before I finally told her of my fear. In addition to telling me how much God loves us, she taught me Bible verses to say when I was fearful. She talked with other mothers of second graders in our church, and together, they made a visit to the Sunday school superintendent. Miss Jones was promoted to the adult division where she didn't have to use fear to maintain discipline.

Through the years, I came to realize that understanding the character of God is the foundation for a productive prayer life.

Understanding the Character of God

Though we can say words designated as a prayer and even have a motive of wanting to communicate with God, there can be no prayer power until we know and trust the One to whom we pray. In retrospect, I realize that this is what my father taught us three children with a game he started to play with us after my second grade Sunday school experience—a game I continued years later with my own grandchildren. It took me a long time to erase the picture of a vengeful God from my mind, but my father's use of this game gradually enabled me to see God as a loving God whom I could trust with my life.

The game would begin when my father would playfully ask us children at almost any time of the day or night, "How much do I love you? This much?" His hands would be open about twelve inches. "No," we would call out loudly. Then he would open his hands and arms a little wider and ask, "This much?" Our "no" would be a little louder this time. "Then how much?" he would ask. Gleefully, we would fling our arms open as wide as we possibly could and say, "You love us this much, no matter what."

"Suppose I have to discipline you because you disobey a rule we have agreed upon," he would say. "Then do I love you this much?" He would open his hands about twelve inches, and we would begin the procedure all over again. Finally, he would ask, "When I need to discipline you, how much do I love you then?" We would fling our arms open wide and say, "You love us this much, no matter what."

"And what does this form?" he would ask seriously as he stood erect with his arms outstretched. "It forms a cross," we would answer. Then he would draw us to him closely and remind us, "There is One who loves you even more than I do, and He will never leave you nor forsake you; and His name is Jesus."

It was much later that I realized that my dad's game was illustrating the unconditional love of God, of which the greatest evidence is the cross of Christ. I am convinced that only when we know the true character of God are we able to trust our entire lives into his keeping and thus experience a meaningful relationship with him through prayer.

Jesus Taught His Disciples to Pray

The disciples desired to have a meaningful relationship with God through prayer. In Luke 11:1, we find the one recorded request they made of Jesus: "Lord, teach us to pray." Remember that these men had been praying in the synagogue most of their lives. They also had been living, eating, and walking with Jesus daily in Judea and Galilee. Obviously, they had learned about the kingdom of God that Jesus proclaimed. They had seen the miracles he had performed—restoring sight to the blind, health to the sick and diseased, joy to the sorrowful, and hope to the discouraged. Yet there must have been something about his prayer life that they didn't understand. How could he be so fatigued after teaching and loving people for many hours and then return from his prayer time energized and empowered? No doubt they noticed a visible change. As good Hebrews, they had been praying for years, but they saw something quite different when Jesus prayed; and they wanted that.

When my husband, Ralph, preached on prayer, he sometimes told the story of going fishing on the Chickamauga Lake when he was serving his first church before we were married. There was an elderly man in his congregation named Mr. Atkinson who had a small fishing boat, and on Ralph's day off, Mr. Atkinson would often call and invite him to go fishing on the Chickamauga Lake, which is part of the Tennessee Valley Authority system. They would put the little boat in the Tennessee River and punt upstream to the Chickamauga Dam. Mr. Newell, the lockmaster, who also was a member of the church, would open the immense gate, and they would tie up on a floating buoy inside the lock. The gate would close and thousands of gallons of water would be taken from the lake and put under their little boat. When the level of the lake was reached, the upper gate would open, and they would go out on a new level into the lake.

To Ralph, this was a simple analogy of what happened to Jesus in his practice of prayer—and what can happen to us through prayer. We can go into our prayer time feeling discouraged, fatigued, or even angry, but once we close the gates to the outside world and really pray, we can emerge on a higher level, seeing our world through different lenses.

Closing the gates to the outside world is not always easy. Most of us rush around doing what comes next, and most of these activities don't turn our thoughts heavenward. I've learned that it helps me to go to the same place each day for prayer. My prayer place is a lounge chair beside my desk, on which rests my Bible and other devotional materials. I close the door to the other part of the house; and when I look outside and see the lake behind our house, I mentally begin to relax. (When I am not at home, I imagine the lake.) Then I center down by closing my eyes, taking three deep breaths, and giving thanks. I'm always surprised at how quickly I can close the gates to the outside world.

How Shall We Pray?

When I read the prayer that Jesus taught his disciples in the first century—and, through the Scriptures, all those who have followed him through the centuries—it seems to me that there are six parts to this prayer. Exploring these parts of the Lord's Prayer can enable us more effectively to understand how to pray.

1. Pray affirmatively

There is nothing tentative about the Lord's Prayer. It is not a doubter's prayer but the prayer of one who believes that "with God all things are possible" (Matthew 19:26 NIV). Jesus didn't instruct us to pray, "God, if you really exist," or "God, I don't know whether you exist or not." Rather, he taught us to pray, "Our Father in heaven" (Matthew 6:9). He gave us a prayer to be prayed by one who confidently knows and trusts the character of God and thus can approach a loving Father.

In his book *O Say Can You See?* James W. Moore tells the story of a little girl who had a cut in the soft flesh of her eyelid (Nashville: Abingdon Press, 2000, p. 83). The doctor knew the child needed some stitches, but he also knew that because of the location of the cut, he shouldn't use an anesthetic. When he talked with the child, he asked if she thought that she could feel the touch of the needle without flinching. The girl thought about it seriously and then declared she believed she could do it if her dad would hold her. When the father took the little girl on his lap, he steadied her head on his shoulder, and everything went perfectly.

Perhaps it was this kind of trust that Jesus meant when he said, "Truly I tell you, whoever does not receive the kingdom of God as a little child will never enter it" (Mark 10:15). This is the kind of trust we exhibit when we trust God as "Our Father who art in heaven."

2. Pray words of praise to the Father

Jesus not only taught us to pray confidently to our loving Father but also instructed us to reverence him, acknowledging his holiness and greatness. "Our Father in heaven, hallowed be your name" (Matthew 6:9). Instead of launching into a litany of pleadings and requests, we need to come first into the presence of our holy, loving, and gracious Father whose blessings we should remember and give thanks for each day.

In the previous chapter, I mentioned the importance of mental focus. Whatever gets our attention, gets us! I realized this truth several years ago when I made an amazing discovery—at least it was new for me. Through the centuries, Christians have spoken of the importance of focusing on God—his holiness, his love, his power, his goodness. Yet, somehow, I had never made this application in a common, everyday experience. Then, one day, I realized that when I focus on a problem for a long time, I grow weary of it and its solution eludes me. But when I give the problem my best thought, turn it loose, and focus on the greatness of God, suddenly a creative solution floods into my mind. That surely must be what the adage "Let go and let God" means. In everyday life, it is so important to focus on God's holiness, greatness, and goodness rather than on our own fears and uncertainties and needs.

For years, I would awaken in the morning with stressful thoughts of all the things I had to do that day. I was tired before I even began. One morning, it became crystal clear to me that God had given me the power to control my thoughts. The words of the apostle Paul in his letter to the Romans confronted me as if they were on a flashing neon sign: "Do not be conformed to this world, but be transformed by the renewing of your minds, so that you may discern what is the will of God" (12:2).

It occurred to me that I can change my day by controlling my thoughts when I awaken. I can change my waking thoughts from stress to strength by focusing on God and counting my blessings instead of my fears. My core personality has changed in these thirty intervening years to make me a person of optimism and hope rather than worry and anxiety.

In our praise to the Father, we need to remember to give thanks for *all* our blessings, including what some might consider "little" blessings. So often we focus on the things we don't have—a new car, a better salary, more appreciation from our colleagues—instead of the little things we take for granted that make life so much more pleasant.

Recently, I read a devotional written by Elizabeth Sherrill (*Daily Guideposts 2008* [New York: Guideposts, 2007], 105). She told of her irritations while making a long trip into the city on a cold, snowy day to go to the dentist. She had to park away from the dentist's office and walk through slush so that her feet were wet and cold. To add to her misery, she had no quarters for the parking meter, so she had to walk another block for the change. By the time she finally arrived at her destination, she was in no mood to find the office door locked. Had she written down the date incorrectly, or was it their fault? She wondered. All she knew was that her feet were cold and she had wasted an entire morning.

After stopping at the ladies' room in the lobby to find some paper towels to dry her feet, she noticed a young woman shaking from the cold and crying. As she struggled between her broken Spanish and the young woman's broken English, she managed to learn that the young woman had been waiting for one hour for a bus that never came.

While driving the woman to her rooming house, she discovered that her passenger had been going to the Immigration Office each day for a week only to be told, "Come back tomorrow." Mostly, however, the young woman talked about her joy at being reunited with her husband, who had been here alone for three years, and about their good fortune in sharing a room with only one other couple. The author said that as she returned to her own husband and their home of many rooms, her irritation at trifles simply melted away.

Jesus teaches us to focus constantly on God and his goodness to us, which lifts our eyes from our petty annoyances to the bounty of his blessings.

3. Pray expectantly, trusting God to meet your needs— and those of others

"Your kingdom come. Your will be done, on earth as it is in heaven. Give us this day our daily bread." It is obvious from these words that Jesus wants us to expect results in prayer. We should expect that we will be different when we come out of our prayer time and that God will meet our needs and the needs of others.

One of my happiest memories as a little girl was visiting my grand-mother, who always went to Sunday school and church on Sunday. As she gave me my bath on Saturday night, she would say with great excite-ment, "Tomorrow is Sunday, and we are going to Sunday school and church." She didn't say, "Hurry up and get your bath because if it doesn't rain tomorrow, we are going to see your Aunt Mary." She made going to Sunday school and church seem like the most exciting experience that could happen to any of us. Even to this day, I have a sense of excitement when I leave our house and head toward Sunday school and worship. I expect to feel God's presence; I expect to learn something; I expect to enjoy the fellowship of the body of Christ.

Jesus must have had something of the same feeling. His relationship with God was so close that he could be still and listen so that he could receive power to handle the pressures of his day and power to forgive oth-ers' sins and draw them closer to God. As we receive God's love and feel his presence, we feel comfortable to pour out our anxieties and needs. We begin to see these needs in the light of his Kingdom purposes. We then seek not to move the arm of God but to be moved by it, for it is in God's purposes that we find our deepest happiness. It's in this period of clarity that we can accept God's answers to our requests, whether they be "yes," "no," or "not yet."

It is also at this time—as we focus on God's Kingdom purposes—that we intercede for others. We bring these persons before the throne of God, praying that they will receive the presence of God in powerful ways. We pray for what we believe are their specific needs. Since God knows their hearts and we don't, we leave them in his care in trust.

I have learned two other things about intercessory prayer. We must learn to listen for things we can do—or not do—to meet others' needs. Our opportunity to be the hands of God gradually becomes clear over a period of time. Sometimes we are to take our hands off completely. This is such an important part of the process that I recommend you keep a prayer journal, noting your prayers, when they were prayed, and how they are answered.

Praying expectantly means trusting God to provide our basic needs, such as our daily bread. In all our needs, we come to expect God to provide abundantly, "far more than all we can ask" (Ephesians 3:20). As we pray for others, we also seek forgiveness for ourselves.

4. Pray with humility and seek forgiveness

Jesus prayed, "And forgive us our debts, as we also have forgiven our debtors" (Matthew 6:12).

The minister who married us told us never to go to bed angry. We moved out of state just after our wedding, so we didn't see the minister again until several years later. We laughingly told him that we stayed up later than ever before that first year of marriage, working through our disagreements. It was good advice—and biblical: "Let not the sun go down upon your wrath" (Ephesians 4:26 KJV). Then when we prayed together, we didn't have a residue of hurt feelings.

In a similar fashion, when we pray and ask God's forgiveness for our mistakes and sins, we make it easier for ourselves to forgive those who have offended us.

5. Pray for protection

Recently, I heard a sermon by Dr. Haddon Robinson, who is the Harold John Ockenga Distinguished Professor for Preaching and the director of the doctoral ministry program at Gordon Conwell Seminary. A Baylor University poll named him as one of the twelve most effective preachers in the English-speaking world. His sermon "Temptation" was from the Genesis story of Eve and the apple. Dr. Robinson pointed out how temptation comes to us in enticing ways—not ugly, repulsive ways. Whether we are tempted by lust, pride, gluttony, apathy, or shaving the truth, we are in danger and need protection. We are to pray, "And lead us not into temptation, but deliver us from evil" (Matthew 6:13 KJV).

Most important, we need to remember God's care for us—and then give him the glory.

6. Give God the glory

We close the prayer by giving God glory: "For thine is the kingdom, and the power, and the glory, for ever. Amen" (Matthew 6:13 KJV). There is no way we can come out of this intimate conversation with our ultimate Friend feeling mean and petty. We receive far more blessings than those we had requested. We receive insight, motivation, love, and what the apostle Paul calls "the peace . . . which surpasses all understanding" (Philippians 4:7). Like the little fishing boat that went from the Tennessee River to Chickamauga Lake, we come out on a higher plane than when we began our prayer time. And our natural response, like that of Jesus, should be to give God the glory.

This was the kind of conversation with the loving Father that allowed Jesus to return to his ministry tasks with renewed energy and power. And the same is equally true for us today.

Praying without Ceasing

In addition to following Jesus' example of how we are to pray in specific times set apart for prayer, we also need to heed the admonition of the apostle Paul to "pray without ceasing" (1 Thessalonians 5:17). This kind of prayer is a running conversation with God throughout the day. It begins with an early morning greeting before getting out of bed: "Good morning, Lord, what are we going to be doing today?" Then, whenever we face a difficult circumstance or person throughout the day, we ask silently, "Lord, what is your approach in this situation?" It is amazing to me how this simple procedure has enabled me to avoid hasty or angry reactions.

All of us know some people who really bug us. They may be relatives, colleagues, or just people who remind us of Aunt Vera or Uncle Joe, both of whom we dislike with a passion. Tom Brown wrote this quatrain in 1680, but it still rings true today:

> I do not like thee, Dr. Fell.
> The reason why, I cannot tell.
> But this I know and know full well.
> I do not like thee, Dr. Fell.

The question is, What do we do? Do we escalate our adversarial relationship through manipulation, verbal punches, or conversations with others about the situation? If we do, we are like Br'er Rabbit in Joel Chandler Harris's Uncle Remus story about Br'er Rabbit and the Tar Baby.

Br'er Fox was feeling that Br'er Rebbit was too confident, so Br'er Fox devised a plan to bring him down to size. Br'er Fox constructed a Tar Baby made of tar and turpentine. He gave him a saucy straw hat to wear and placed him in the middle of the road by which Br'er Rabbit would travel. Br'er Rabbit was incensed when he greeted Tar Baby cheerily and received no reply. Still, he made two more civil attempts to talk with Tar Baby. When he was ignored, he became furious and began to react.

First, he took a punch at Tar Baby's jaw, and his hand stuck to the tar. Growing increasingly frustrated, he punched with another hand, kicked with both feet, and then butted with his head. Of course, he was hopelessly and humiliatingly stuck to his adversary until Br'er Fox threw him into the briar patch. There he was torn loose in painful ways.

In my own life, I have learned that it is not helpful to react to the person who is an irritant. Instead of trying to change someone, which we cannot do, and self-destructing in the process, we must recognize that every individual has a right to his or her opinions. Trying to prove someone wrong is an exercise in futility and a waste of our own energy. Neither should we allow him or her to dominate our thoughts and actions. In fact, we must limit our contact with the person as much as possible.

So, what can we do? If there is something that has caused a rift in our relationship and we can talk it through, we must do it and then forgive the person. Otherwise, we will be tied to that person forever. "Agree with [your] adversary quickly" (Matthew 5:25 KJV) is good advice because the longer we wait, the greater the risk becomes.

I know of a woman who was upset with her sister over the fact that their deceased mother left a bit more money to the sister than she left to her (less than $100). It was only after this woman became ill from the long-held resentment that she was willing to admit to her sister the cause of the rift. If she could have done this quickly, how many hard feelings and misunderstandings could have been avoided? Forgiveness could have restored family unity.

If the problem is simply a personality conflict, there are three things we can do. Instead of *reacting*, try these three positive *responses* the next time you are irritated by another person.

1. Turn the person loose from your thoughts

You must not allow the person to dominate space in your mind that could be used for creative, productive thoughts. This is easier said than done, particularly if you have to work or live with the individual.

If you are working with a difficult person, learn to be civil. Stay away from gossip about that person, and don't try constantly to curry favor with him or her. That's like throwing meat to a hungry dog. However, an occasional and unexpected kindness—such as an offer to help with the person's workload when you are caught up with your own—may pay big dividends. I have learned that difficult people often have been deeply hurt and thus feel the need to hurt others. The unexpected kindness will sometimes defuse the need—at least temporarily.

If the difficult person is one you live with, you need to set some boundaries. I once heard Joyce Landorf, an author and speaker, say how she tried for years to get approval from a member of her family of origin and continued to be hurt by his rejection. The maid told her that there were some irregular foods in the grocery store and that her difficult person was irregular. "Of course, he is not going to change," the maid told her, "so don't spend your life trying to make that happen. God has given you your life to live, so live to his glory!" This is good advice to heed when we are dealing with somebody incapable of or unwilling to give approval.

2. Remember that every person has some good traits

Begin to look for these good traits in the other person. When possible, compliment or help the person. For example, if the individual has received a promotion or his or her children have received special honors, offer sincere congratulations. If there is something you can do to be of genuine help in a project, or something you can say at the death of a loved one, say it or do it sincerely. In this way, over a period of time, you can wear away feelings of irritation or hostility.

One of my happiest friendships now is with a lady who once worked with me on a church committee. We had a big job to accomplish and needed every committee member to work together. She seemed to oppose every suggestion I made and even sabotaged some of our progress. I was ready for a full-fledged confrontation, but in my prayer time, I felt led to look for things I could praise about her contributions. I even offered to help when her part of the project wasn't finished in time. Admittedly, I didn't really *want* to do that; I felt *led* to do it. But what an amazing turnaround occurred in her attitude. Years later, she told me that she was upset because she felt that people were listening to my suggestions more than hers. Here was a potential enemy who became a dear friend.

3. Pray for the person

I've learned that when I pray for others, more happens to me than to them. Eventually, I'm set free. Try it! It's far superior to being in bondage to an adversarial relationship.

Dr. Frank Laubach is perhaps best known for his plan for global literacy, "Each One Teach One." In addition, he is well known as a strong Christian who understood prayer power and who suggested the idea of "shooting" prayers toward others. It is an exciting experiment! I have used it in church, on planes, in the grocery store, and in other public places with some surprising results.

Dr. Norman Vincent Peale wrote an article that appeared in *Plus* magazine a number of years ago in which he shared a personal example of the power of shooting prayers. He said that once he was in a barber shop in Switzerland, and the barber spoke very good English because he had cut hair for GIs during World War II. A woman sat in the chair next to his. She was middle aged and appeared angry—even full of hate. Since most people were speaking Swiss-German or French, the woman said loudly,

"Doesn't anybody in this crummy shop speak English?" The woman in charge said, "I have a nice little girl who speaks English. I will bring her to you."

The young girl spoke only a few words of English, so the American woman compensated by speaking more loudly: "This is the way I have my hair done in New York, and I want it done that way here. I want two little curls at each side to soften my face." The barber whispered to Dr. Peale, "It would take more than curls to soften that battle ax's face."

Dr. Peale said that he was ashamed that an American would behave like that. Then the idea came to him, "This is no way to be thinking of her. Let me try the power of thought and shooting prayers." He began to shoot prayers such as, "Lord, this is one of your creations. She has a beautiful soul, but she isn't showing it now. Give her a calm sense of your presence and bless her."

Shortly, the woman turned to Dr. Peale and asked, "Do you speak English?" Dr. Peale replied, "A little, Madame." The woman continued, "I am an unhappy woman, and I have had a lot of terrible things happen to me. I know I sound mean, but I'm not as mean as I sound." Suddenly, the woman gave them a beautiful smile.

The barber whispered to Dr. Peale, "What in heaven's name did you do to that woman? I need to know because I deal with people like her all the time." When Dr. Peale explained that he had shot her with prayerful thoughts of love and respect, the barber was amazed at what he had seen happen. (From "Activate Your Personality Power," *Plus* magazine, vol. 46, number 8 [October 1995]: part 1, 6–8.)

Try using the power of shooting prayers, rather than thinking thoughts of irritation and condemnation. At the very least, it will make you more aware of others. At best, you will be used to bless others in subtle but powerful ways. Remember, we are blessed to be a blessing!

A Final Note

I can't conclude this chapter on prayer without mentioning how often people say to me, "What can you do when your prayer is not answered?" I usually quote Bill Hybels, senior pastor of Willow Creek Church, who says that God always answers prayer with one of four replies:

1. "No"—inappropriate request
2. "Slow"—work carefully in that situation
3. "Grow"—you need to grow before the time is right
4. "Go"—the request is appropriate, the time is right, and you are prepared to handle the situation carefully
(From the "Living Faith" series, Nightingale Conant [www.Nightingale.com])

When the request is appropriate, the time is right, and you are prepared to handle the situation carefully, God always says, "Go for it!"

Digging a Little Deeper

1. Why is understanding the character of God so important to prayer? How has your understanding of God changed through the years?
2. Recall the analogy of the little boat that was lifted from the river to the lake, going out on a higher level. How does the same thing happen to us in prayer?
3. Read the Lord's Prayer in Matthew 6:9-13. In what ways is the prayer Jesus taught his disciples a pattern for our prayers?
4. *Our Father in heaven.* Why do you think Jesus began the prayer with "Our father" rather than "My father"? What does this tell us about the nature of God? Prayer should lift us beyond our personal quest and give

us confidence in the fact that God hears and answers. What, in this section of the prayer, causes us to do that?

5. *"Hallowed be your name"* (Matthew 6:9). Why is it important for us to focus immediately on God's holiness, power, and goodness rather than on a list of our needs?

6. *"Your kingdom come. Your will be done, on earth as it is in heaven. Give us this day our daily bread"* (Matthew 6:10-11). Why is it important for us to see our needs in light of God's kingdom here on earth? In what places and ways are you currently working for God's kingdom on earth?

7. Why does interceding for others help us to understand them and their needs more completely?

8. *"Forgive us our debts, as we also have forgiven our debtors"* (Matthew 6:12). Why do you think Jesus placed such an emphasis on our need to forgive?

9. All of us face temptation from time to time. At this point in your life, what is your greatest struggle, and how do you most need God's protection and help?

10. *"For thine is the kingdom, and the power, and the glory, for ever"* (Matthew 6:13 KJV). Why do you think Jesus ended this model prayer with an acknowledgment of the power and majesty of God? Why is it impossible for our prayers to be effective if they are totally self-centered (my needs, my requests, my pain)? How does acknowledging the power of God help us to feel empowered and full of hope?

CHAPTER NINE

Choose Christ, Not Chaos

And I, when I am lifted up from the earth, will draw
all people to myself. (John 12:32)

I t was on a bench in the Lake District of Great Britain in the summer of 1986 that my husband, Ralph, and I rediscovered the amazing power of Christ to bring hope, direction, and happiness into our otherwise chaotic lives.

At the time, we were taking part in a six-week ministerial pulpit exchange with a Methodist pastor in West Kirby, England—a resort town across the Mersey River from Liverpool. That pastor and his wife had flown to our city in East Tennessee to live in our parsonage and take up the responsibilities as senior pastor of our church. We had done the same for them. Thus far, it had been a delightful experience! In only a few weeks, we had begun to think more like Brits as we read their newspapers and listened to the BBC.

The wonderful church members had done everything possible to make our visit memorable. For example, we had arrived in West Kirby during the last week of June. On the following Sunday, the church's chairman of the board had announced a luncheon for all members and guests to be held later that week. On the way to the church that day, we had commented that it was the Fourth of July and that our friends and family back home would be celebrating. Imagine our surprise when we walked into the church's dining hall to see that the entire room had been decorated in red, white, and blue with a huge American flag, borrowed from a nearby air base, on display in the center of the room. The music of the day had featured American patriotic songs, including our national anthem. Those thoughtful people had made that Fourth of July holiday one we will never forget. I jokingly told some of them later that if their countrymen had been that generous in 1776, we might still be British!

Another generous gesture of the church members had been their insistence that we take two or three days each week to visit nearby sites, including the flower festival in Liverpool, the decoration of the wells in Sheffield, the city of London, and the Lake District in northwest England. The latter I had starred in our itinerary as one of the places I had hoped to visit. I had wanted to see Beatrice Potter's home and visit the gift shop there because we had used her children's books and china for our sons when they were small. I had admired her gift of storytelling, which had so delighted our children. Also, having been an English major in college, I especially liked the works of William Wordsworth. To see the home of his birth and visit his grave would be a literary treat for me.

So we had decided to spend the night in a little hotel in Grasmere. Little had I realized that this small village would be the scene of a deeply spiritual experience for us.

God Comes to Us in Unexpected Ways

Though I would not realize it until later, God had prepared us for the experience in Grasmere in advance by coming to us in an unexpected way. Before I say more about this, you need to understand my state of mind during the time we were in England. Ralph's plan to retire from active ministry the following year—a year before our denomination's compulsory retirement age, which we thought was much too young—had been troubling me. Where would we live, what would we do to serve God, and how would we save enough money to take care of us during our retirement years? After all, the minister's pension in our area was small. These worries had been tugging at my mind like a dog after a bone.

Part of the answer came in finding an unexpected book in the English pastor's library. Because we had had so many items to pack for our trip, we had not brought a devotional book, feeling confident that our colleague would have one in his library. Yet after our arrival, we had not been able to find a single one. We had discovered, however, a book entitled *The Positive Power of Jesus Christ* by Norman Vincent Peale, which neither of us had read. So we had decided to use this book for our devotions each day.

Both of us were familiar with Peale's work. In my early days of parenting a colicky baby, I had overcome my negativism and discouragement by reading and applying Peale's plan of action outlined in one of his earliest books, *A Guide to Confident Living*. For me, it had served as a very practical action plan for changing my life by renewing my mind. Later, Ralph and I had read his bestseller *The Power of Positive Thinking*. Yet neither of those books seemed to have the depth of faith that we found in *The Positive Power of Jesus Christ*. As we would soon discover, this book would serve as a directional sign pointing us toward the future.

Because we were reading *The Positive Power of Jesus Christ* while living in England, we were reminded of the words that King George VI had delivered in his Christmas radio address in 1943 as the country had braced for the onslaught of the Nazis during World War II. To an anxious and overstressed nation, he had quoted the words of English poet Minnie Louisa Haskin:

> I said to the man who stood at the gate of the year,
> "Give me a light that I might tread safely into the unknown."
> And he replied, "Put your hand into the hand of God.
> That should be to you better than a light
> And safer than a known way."
> ("The Gate of the Year," published by Hodder & Stoughton: London, 1940)

As we prepared for a new phase in life, Ralph and I were treading into the unknown, and Dr. Peale's book reminded us that God would guide us. In fact, we would soon discover that part of Dr. Peale's story would have amazing similarities to our spiritual experience in England. To help you understand this experience and its implications for our future, let me pause to share Dr. Peale's story with you—a story that beautifully illustrates God's guidance in our lives.

God Comes to Us When We Need Guidance

A youthful Norman Vincent Peale, having graduated from Boston University School of Theology and having married the love of his life, Ruth Stafford, was in his fifth year as senior pastor of the University Avenue Methodist Church in Syracuse, New York. Those were exciting years for both of the Peales, and they never once thought of moving.

Then, in a short period of time, the young pastor received invitations to serve as pastor of two different churches. The first came from First Methodist Church in Los Angeles, California. At the time, this was the largest church in the Methodist denomination. The second invitation was from the oldest Protestant church in America, Marble Collegiate Reformed Church in New York City, established in 1628. It had a long and illustrious history, and many distinguished clergymen had served there. Since the beloved Daniel Poling, who had served effectively as pastor, had resigned three years earlier, the membership had been reduced to five hundred persons; and attendance at both morning and evening services had dwindled to about two hundred at each service. They needed help!

Wishing earnestly to do what God wanted them to do, the Peales wrote down the pros and cons of going to each of the churches, and then they prayed individually for guidance for thirty days. When no decision had been reached by this time, Ruth declared, "We are going into a prayer time together and won't emerge until a decision is made." In commenting on this incident, her husband wrote that she was a sweet and gentle person who, on occasion, could be firm, unyielding, and tough. She obviously was a "can do" person who knew that, for the sake of the churches and for their own peace of mind, a decision needed to be made.

They agreed to pray for discernment until they received God's answer. After a two-and-a-half-hour prayer vigil, the pastor asked his wife if she had received an answer. She nodded affirmatively. "What is it?" he inquired. "What answer did you get?" She didn't tell him, feeling that, because he was the pastor, the answer had to be his. He replied that he had received an answer and felt that it definitely was from God. "Go to New York" was the message. Ruth had received the same message! And history gives testimony of the glorious results of their obedience to God's direction.

God Comes to Us When Our Circumstances Are Discouraging

Eventually, the two morning services at Marble Collegiate Church were filled to capacity, with overflow crowds watching the services by closed circuit television. Norman Vincent Peale's prolific writing, speaking, and national radio broadcasts brought scores of visitors every Sunday to the stately edifice on Fifth Avenue and Nineteenth Street in New York City.

However, the beginning of Peale's ministry at Marble Collegiate Church had been difficult, and the growth had come slowly and incrementally. This was partly due to the social condition of the country at the time. The United States was in the midst of the worst financial and economic depression in its history. Although we have had several financial recessions since then, we have experienced nothing like the Great Depression. The depression affected all of America, but New York, the financial capital of the nation, felt it the hardest. Thousands walked the streets futilely looking for jobs. There were bread lines and business and factory closings almost daily.

Throughout the depression, Norman Vincent Peale preached about opportunity in the midst of difficulties. His sermons centered on the theme "man's extremity is God's opportunity," a phrase Dr. Peale attributed to Anglican pastor Thomas Adams, who was sometimes called the Shakespeare of Puritan theology. (This same phrase was later used regularly by English pastor and author Charles Spurgeon, as well as Peter Marshall, the renowned American pastor from Scotland.) To the discouraged, depressed, and even hopeless people of his day, Peale began to preach a positive message that God loved them and would help them no matter how bad things became. As people heard and received this positive and hopeful message, the church began to grow. The congregation was getting it!

Even so, the young pastor had a tendency toward self-doubt. He found that the gloom and stress of his situation—ministering to discouraged, depressed, and hopeless people in a very difficult time—was having an almost paralyzing effect on his thinking. It had seeped pervasively into his mind and discolored it. When he and his wife took their first vacation after going to Marble Collegiate Church, they went to Keswick in the Lake District of England. Each day after taking a walk, they would sit on one of the benches in the formal garden. Daily, the pastor would pour out his woes to his young wife.

Ruth listened patiently for several days to her husband's diatribe, and then one day, she went into what he called her tough mode. She told him that he preached about God's power and love but wasn't acting as if he had faith in anything he was preaching. Reminiscent of her resolve when seeking God's guidance concerning which church they should serve, she said that they weren't going to get up off that bench until he surrendered to the Lord all the things that were disturbing him—the church, the situation in the nation, and the discouragement of his mind. Peale did just that, and he later reported, "Such peace as I would have never believed possible surged through me, and with it a burst of joy."

He was elated and ready to return to New York and to work. It is reported that his life was never the same from that moment on.

The Peales' experience at Keswick has a message for us all: When life is hard and our circumstances are discouraging, let's remember that our extremity—that place where we are at the end of our rope—is God's opportunity. We can expect to have some guidance and peace when we surrender all our circumstances to God. Ralph and I remembered this lesson from the Peales while we were in England, and God connected the dots into our own future.

God Comes to Us to "Connect the Dots"

About fifty years after the Peales sat on that bench in Keswick, Ralph and I arrived at Grasmere, another location in the Lake District of England. First, we visited Beatrice Potter's home and gift shop. After dinner at our small hotel, we found Wordsworth's grave and read some of his poetry. Then, we took a stroll through that quaint but charming village. We stopped momentarily to sit on a bench, observing the beauty all around us. It was then that we both came to the same conclusion: God had providentially provided the very book we had needed for a time of uncertainty in our lives. God also had provided a place of quiet reflection—a solitary bench in beautiful Grasmere—where we could sift through the uncertainties of an impending retirement period.

Having read what had happened in a similar situation for a couple whose ministry we admired, it was easy for us to follow the instructions of Proverbs 3:5-6: "Trust in the LORD with all your heart, and do not rely on your own insight. In all your ways acknowledge him, and he will make straight your paths." We were willing to verbalize honestly to God our concerns and fears about what might happen after retirement. And most important, we understood that we needed a rededication of our lives, our ministry, and our hopes for the future to Christ, our Lord.

As we did this in complete trust that God "is able to do exceeding abundantly above all that we ask or think, according to the power that worketh in us" (Ephesians 3:20 KJV), the miracle happened! We had peace about the future, courage for the present, and joy for the journey.

We returned to our church in East Tennessee with excitement about what could be done before we left the church because we weren't overburdened by worry. In January of the following year, Ralph announced his intention to retire in June. A little over a week after his announcement, we received an invitation for both of us to join the staff of one of the national boards of our denomination. Those positions provided opportunities for us to travel, speak, and write—things we never could have done to that degree while serving a church. We serve an awesome God!

The Choice Is Ours

As for happiness—choosing Christ, I believe, is not only the way to avoid chaos; it is the ultimate key to lasting happiness.

Has it occurred to you how much of life is determined by our choice? We choose our thoughts, our beliefs, our actions, our friends, and our use of resources. We are not victims! We have been given the incomparable gift of choice by the God who loves us and stands ready to empower us. God never overrides us; the choice is always ours. Let us choose Christ—and happiness—each and every day!

Digging a Little Deeper

1. Describe a time when there was chaos and/or uncertainty in your life. How did your faith help you at that time?
2. Read John 12:32. What does it mean to "lift up" Christ in our daily lives? What are some ways we can do this?
3. Do you believe it was an accident or God's providence that enabled us to find Norman Vincent Peale's book in the English pastor's library?

Why do you believe this? Have you ever experienced God's providential activity in your life? If so, when and how has God come to you in unexpected ways?

4. When the Peales were seeking discernment to know God's will, why do you think that praying together proved to be more effective than praying individually? Do you believe that carefully thinking through the decision individually prepared the way for them to receive the same answer when they prayed together? Why or why not?

5. Other than individual and joint or corporate prayer, what else do you do when seeking discernment to know God's will? How can we know when God is speaking to us?

6. Describe a time when you felt really discouraged. Did you wallow in your depressing thoughts or surrender your worries to God? Why do you think we find it hard to surrender every part of ourselves to God?

7. If trying to be our own anchor ends in frustration and fragmentation, what happens when we allow Christ to be our anchor?

8. Read Proverbs 3:5-6. How is trusting in the Lord different from leaning on our own understanding? Tell of a time in your own life when you followed the instructions of these verses.

9. Read Ephesians 3:20. What is the power that works in us? When have you found these words to be true in your own life? Explain.

10. What does choosing Christ have to do with authentic and lasting happiness? How can we choose Christ each and every day?

CHAPTER TEN

Choose the Secret of Happiness and Power

[Paul] said to them, "Did you receive the Holy Spirit when you became believers?" They replied, "No, we have not even heard that there is a Holy Spirit." (Acts 19:2)

This final chapter is the one I almost didn't write because there is so much misunderstanding about the Holy Spirit. Yet each time I tried to close the book without it, I felt such "divine discontent" that I knew I had to include it. We need to be reminded of the power of the Holy Spirit within us. When I think of discovering the power of the Holy Spirit within us, I think of my friend Sarah.

Sarah and I were classmates in college. She was a tall, slender, attractive brunette—and she was smart. If anyone in our dorm needed help with calculus or French, we went straight to room 101, and Sarah patiently worked us through it. Yet, with all of her good looks and intelligence, she was one of the most insecure persons I've ever met. She was extremely fearful, always expecting the worst to happen.

Usually in our late-night relaxation times of food and laughter, Sarah never seemed to relax. There was an inner tension about her that made others uncomfortable. Even after graduation, I often wondered about the paradox in the life of my smart and beautiful classmate. I didn't see her again until I returned to the campus for a class reunion twenty-five years later. She was a transformed person—calm, relaxed, and radiating peace with herself and others. When we were alone, I said, "You are a different person from the one I knew in college. What has happened?" When she told me something of the dysfunctional family in which she grew up, I better understood her insecurities. But what had turned her around?

She explained it this way:

> First, I fell in love with and married a truly wonderful, Christian man who loved me unconditionally. Yet because of my insecurities, I found it hard to trust him. It was hard for me to believe that anyone really loved me. I must have tested his Christian faith to the limit. But I saw in him peace and joy that I longed for. Little by little, I began to see the difference in our faiths. Though I had attended confirmation class and had joined the church when I was twelve, my faith didn't help me in daily living—except in broad moral values. Even then, I felt as if I could never measure up.
>
> Jim's faith was a relationship with Jesus. Through the Holy Spirit, Christ lives within Jim. He turns to this Holy Guest for guidance, comfort, help in times of temptation, and strength for each day's journey. This empowers him with confidence, joy, and peace.
>
> I, on the other hand, was like the early Christians in Ephesus. In answer to Paul's question, "Did you receive the Holy Spirit when you became believers?" they answered, "No. We didn't even know there is a Holy Spirit." When I learned of a class on the Holy Spirit to be held in our church, I quickly enrolled.

I looked at the radiant woman before me and thought of the insecure, negative girl I had known in college. I shall always remember what she said next: "Nell, I believe the secret of happiness and power comes from opening our lives to the Holy Spirit."

As I watched Sarah that day, I concluded that she is a living example of an illustration a minister once used in speaking of the Holy Spirit. He told of a Native American man whose wagon was drawn by a team of white horses as he made his weekly pilgrimage into the nearest town. When oil was discovered within the reservation, material possessions became more accessible to members of the tribe. The man bought a long, shiny, new Cadillac. On Saturday, the man called for his team of white horses to be attached to his new car, and slowly, they made their way into town. Under the hood of his car was a hundred times more power than he had in his team of horses, but he didn't know it. He didn't understand how to use his new purchase.

That's what had happened to Sarah—and what happens to many of us Christians. We are full of tension and insecurities when we insist on dragging our problem-laden lives along without recognizing the power latent within us through the Holy Spirit. Certainly, we need to learn more about this third person in the Holy Trinity.

Who Is the Holy Spirit?

In the first chapter of this book, I wrote that the incarnation means "in Christ God was reconciling the world to himself" (2 Corinthians 5:19). Then, as Christ becomes resident within us through the Holy Spirit, we receive guidance. Before he died, Jesus told his disciples: "If you love me, you will keep my commandments. And I will ask the Father, and he will give you another Advocate, to be with you forever. This is the Spirit of truth [Holy Spirit], whom the world cannot receive, because it neither sees him nor knows him. You know him, because he abides with you, and he will be in you" (John 14:15-17).

Remember that it was fifty days after the resurrection when the believers were waiting in Jerusalem and, just as Jesus promised, the Holy Spirit descended upon them. He came with power in the sound of a mighty, rushing wind and tongues of fire; and suddenly, each believer had the ability to speak in another language. The disciples who had been filled with fear at the crucifixion now became courageous and visionary. They were empowered, and the Christian church was born (Acts 2:1-4).

The Holy Spirit is the third person in the Trinity: God, the Father; Jesus, the Son; and the Holy Spirit. In 2 Corinthians 13:13, Paul defines the doctrine of the Trinity in his beautiful benediction: "The grace of the Lord Jesus Christ, the love of God, and the communion of the Holy Spirit be with all of you."

Just as we, individually, are one entity with three parts—body, mind, and spirit—so also is the triune God. God the creator is the mind; Jesus, who lived on the earth, is the body; and the Holy Spirit is the Risen Christ living within us. Another way of explaining the Trinity is that God the Father created us in his own image (Genesis 1:27), but we all have broken the image (Romans 3:23); Jesus the Son came to earth to redeem us (John 3:16); and the Holy Spirit lives within us to empower us (John 1:12).

In the early church, the followers not only understood the doctrine of the Holy Spirit but also lived under the Holy Spirit's guidance. As the church became more institutionalized, there was less and less understanding of the work of the Holy Spirit.

In a sermon he gave in 1975, the late Bishop Earl G. Hunt said, "There is a hunger on the part of the people around the world for an understanding of the doctrine of the Holy Spirit." Then he went on to say that, unfortunately, we as Protestants, because of our fear of emotionalism, let the doctrine of the Holy Spirit go by default to the Pentecostals. As a result, we have often lost power and vitality in our worship.

So, in order to maintain a vibrant faith, we need to ask how the Holy Spirit fits into our lives.

How Does the Holy Spirit Fit into Our Lives?

In his journal, John Wesley describes grace as having three components: (1) prevenient grace, which goes before us to bring us to faith; (2) justifying grace, whereby we receive forgiveness, salvation, and eternal life when we repent and ask for forgiveness; and (3) sanctifying grace, which means that day by day we are being made perfect in love and motives. This, by the way, does not mean that we are being made perfect in actions. We continue to make mistakes because we are Christians under construction. During the years in which I had an office at the church, there was a sign on my wall that said, "Be patient with me. God hasn't finished with me yet."

Wesley depicted the three components of grace in graphic form using this description. He said that prevenient grace is the path leading to our spiritual house on which God pursues us. Justifying grace is the porch of the house where we receive God's forgiveness of sin and accept Christ as Lord and Savior of our lives. Sanctifying grace is the inside of the house where we open every room of our lives to the Holy Spirit. Let's consider each of the components of grace: prevenient grace, justifying grace, and sanctifying grace.

1. Prevenient grace

God allows each of us to choose to come to faith in him or to reject Him. He does, however, pursue us in gentle and loving ways.

Francis Thompson, English poet of the nineteenth century, said this in his poem "The Hound of Heaven":

> I fled him down the nights and down the days.
> I fled him down the arches of the years.
> I fled him down the labyrinthian ways of my own mind,
>   And in the midst of tears I hid from him,
>   And under running laughter.

Thompson had felt the tug of the Holy Spirit to lead him to the Christian faith, but he wanted to live life in his own way. After college and medical school, his passion became writing poetry. Unfortunately, in those years, he had a growing addiction to drugs, particularly opium. In fact, his addiction grew so severe that he became homeless for several years. A Christian couple, Milford and Alice Maynell, editors of the literary magazine *Merry England*, had seen and liked Thompson's poetry. They worked successfully to get his first book published. At the same time, they cared for Thompson during his drug rehabilitation, encouraged his writing, and eventually led him to faith in Christ.

Thompson's life demonstrates that the Holy Spirit goes before us and pursues us through prevenient grace.

2. Justifying grace

This is the grace that brings us to faith and salvation. In my own life, I fought against this grace. Oh, I loved the church and our youth program, but I was angry with God for not stopping my father's drinking. As a result, I wouldn't join the church with my confirmation class despite appeals from my minister, my parents, and even my own heart.

The summer I was fourteen, I went to a church camp sponsored by our annual conference. There, I met a counselor who was all I wanted to be and wasn't. She was pretty, fun-loving, popular, and a superb athlete. Perhaps sensing my shyness and rebellion, she sought me out, and I loved talking with her. I even took her class in canoeing. One day, I told her about my faith dilemma. She listened sensitively and then led me step by step into a faith commitment to Jesus Christ. It was a very emotional experience for me, and it is still a highlight of my faith journey.

3. Sanctifying grace

This is the grace that accepts us as we are but loves us too much to leave us that way. Our role is to open the rooms of our lives so that the Holy Spirit can heal the broken places and motivate us to leave places where we are stuck.

My college classmate, Sarah, whom you met at the beginning of this chapter, spent a long time allowing the Holy Spirit's sanctifying grace to heal the memories of a terrible childhood. Likewise, each of us must open every room in our spiritual house to the sanctifying work of the Holy Spirit.

First, we must open the library of our minds to the Holy Guest: "And you will know the truth, and the truth will make you free" (John 8:32). We must open the dining room of our appetites—food, drink, sex, ego: "I appeal to you therefore, brothers and sisters, by the mercies of God, to present your bodies as a living sacrifice, holy and acceptable to God, which is your spiritual worship" (Romans 12:1). We must open the living room of our family life, choosing to live in commitment, respect, and unconditional love and encouraging each family member to be all that

God created him or her to be. And we must open the playroom of our social contacts, as well as the study or office of our workplace.

Unfortunately, too often we grant the Holy Spirit entrance into only one room: the parlor, which represents formalized religion. Thus we exclude the Holy Spirit from our everyday living. We have a religion but not a relationship with our living Lord.

When we invite the Holy Spirit to live within us, he is at work even when we are not aware of it—even when we make wrong choices and mistakes. The Bible verse I like to recall when I am disappointed in my thoughts or actions is Philippians 1:6: "I am confident of this, that the one who began a good work among you will bring it to completion by the day of Jesus Christ." Let's consider some practical ways in which this Holy Guest lives and works within us.

How Does the Holy Spirit Work within Us?

If we are believers, the Holy Spirit works within us in our minds, our emotions, and our spirits. Let me suggest a few of the ways in which the Spirit works.

1. The Holy Spirit assures us of our salvation

Many people seek to come into the circle of faith through repentance, asking for forgiveness, and receiving acceptance by God through their belief in Christ. Yet some people find it hard to believe in justifying grace, whereby we receive not only forgiveness but also salvation, the Holy Spirit, and eternal life.

From the time John Wesley was a student at Oxford University, he diligently kept the Holy Habits—daily scripture reading, prayer, worship, and service to others. Yet it was not until he came into a personal relationship with Jesus Christ that he had the assurance of salvation. While attending a Bible study on May 24, 1738, he felt his heart "strangely warmed" and received assurance of his salvation.

In one of the young adult Sunday school classes I taught, there was a handsome man in his late thirties named Bill (not his real name). He was moving up the corporate ladder and was a good husband and father. When he was in his late twenties, his father had asked Bill to give him some help with his will. Knowing that he was his father's favorite, Bill had not protested when his father revealed that he was leaving Bill twice the amount he was leaving his other sons. Bill knew it wasn't right, but he never said a word.

Bill's father died soon after their meeting, and Bill's brother was incensed about the will. He accused Bill of manipulation. Bill tried to convince him of the truth, and he even wrote his brother a check for the amount he should have received. But his brother would have none of it. He sued Bill and said some terrible things about him in the newspaper. Unfortunately, the judge decided in Bill's favor, and the family rift continued.

Bill felt so guilty that he didn't feel worthy of being accepted by Christ. Finally, under great conviction, he came to faith in Christ, but he had no assurance of salvation. We had talked about it many times, but one day I asked, "Bill, did you ever murder anyone?"

Stunned, he replied, "Of course not. I would never do that."

Then I reminded him that the apostle Paul had done just that, and God forgave him and used him mightily in God's work. "If God can do that for Paul," I said, "don't you think he has done that for you? You have done all you can to rectify the situation." You see, I knew that Bill had used the money from his father's will to set up a college fund for his brother's daughter.

"You need to forgive yourself and let God take care of your brother," I told him.

Somehow Bill heard those words, and God has used him mightily since. It took several years for his brother to come around, but today they are united as a family.

2. The Holy Spirit guides us

The Holy Spirit within us serves as a guide, helping us to discern right from wrong, assisting us when we are tempted, enlightening us at the point of decision, and strengthening us in times of crisis. In my experience, this happens with a strong inner assurance of the right answer. You no longer debate the issue.

Recently, I had such clear guidance about the choice of a person to lead music for a women's conference in our church. Since the music needed to be upbeat and a combination of hymns and praise music, we had several persons from whom to choose. The co-chair of the conference and I decided to pray about the decision. In the middle of the night, I was awakened with the name of a person as if it were written on a neon sign.

Early the next morning, I called my friend and said, "I have a name." Quickly she replied, "So do I." We both had received the same name, and we knew that we had received guidance from the Holy Spirit in a practical manner. Confirmation of the guidance came when music for the conference turned out to be far more glorious than we had even hoped.

3. The Holy Spirit instructs us through scripture and worship

Have you ever read scripture, even familiar scripture, and it seemed to leap off the page at you? It is almost as if the words were saying, "This is for you now!" Our job is to read the Scriptures slowly and expect that when the words jump off the page, the Holy Spirit will bring to our remembrance the past or present events that need attention. This can happen privately or when we worship with others.

In 1964, when Russia was just being fully opened up for tourists, Ralph and I went to Moscow. Though our accommodations were far below what they would be today, we were thrilled to enjoy some of the tourist attractions we had only read about—the Kremlin, the University of Moscow, Russian ballet and opera, Lenin's tomb, and many others. Because we were there on a Sunday, we asked our guide to take us to a church. We had read that there were a few Russian Orthodox congregations open and one Protestant, English-speaking church established by the American Baptists. Our guide told us that, as a member of the Communist Party, she was not allowed to go to church. She said, "Besides, you will only find old women attending." She was almost right on that.

I am not sure what instructions she gave our cab driver, but we ended up at a Russian Orthodox Church, not the English-speaking church. Though we understood none of the language, the hymn tunes were familiar, so we sang lustily in English. As the priest read the scripture, I knew it was the parable of the prodigal son. I'm not sure how I knew that unless it was the cadence of his speech or that he had inserted some English words. At the end of the service, when I thanked him for including a little English in the Scripture, he said in fairly good English, "No, I didn't do that." So I asked, "Well, how did I understand the scripture?" The priest replied, "It was the Holy Spirit who instructed you."

We need always to expect the Holy Spirit to inspire our reading and hearing of God's word.

4. The Holy Spirit rescues and empowers us

As I have reflected on my conversation with the Russian Orthodox priest in Moscow, I have become quite certain that when we find ourselves in over our heads, the Holy Spirit rescues and empowers us.

Several years ago, I had written on my calendar, "Speak to volunteers at Siskin Children's Institute." I had diligently prepared my speech, being sure that what I had to say was different from what I had said to them for each of the past four years. The group looked different when I walked in, and I thought they must have recruited lots of new volunteers.

The person who introduced me ended her remarks with these words: "We are so happy to have Nell Mohney here to speak to all of the kindergarten teachers in Hamilton County." I almost fainted! Nothing I had prepared was appropriate for this group. Evidently when the invitation was given, I had assumed that because the place was the same, the group I would be speaking to would be the same as in past years. I prayed my emergency prayer: "Lord, I can't. You can! Please do. Thanks!" As I walked toward the lectern, the Holy Spirit brought to my remembrance a speech I had given in another city to pre-school teachers. Even the illustrations were crystal clear. "Thank you, Lord!" I fairly shouted in my spirit as I returned to my seat.

I know that wouldn't happen on a regular basis. God expects us to have disciplined minds and to prepare. But when we do our best, we can leave the rest to God.

One of the most spectacular rescues recorded in the New Testament is that of the apostle Peter (Acts 12:1-19). After the resurrection, King Herod, in order to stay in good favor with Jewish leaders, had James, the brother of John, killed and Peter arrested. Herod had planned to keep Peter incarcerated until the Feast of the Passover ended. Then he would turn Peter over to the Jewish leaders. On the night before the Passover ended, God sent an angel into the prison, and the chains fell from Peter. The angel asked Peter to get his sandals and wrap and come quickly. Peter thought he was dreaming, but once he was outside, the angel left him, and he knew that he truly had been rescued by God.

That evening, the disciples were meeting at the home of Mary, the mother of John Mark, for an all-night prayer meeting, asking God to rescue Peter. When Peter arrived at the gate of Mary's home, they couldn't believe the good news. Even Rhoda, the maid who answered the knocking at the door, recognized Peter's voice; but she was so excited that she ran to tell the others and left Peter standing outside. There was great rejoicing when Peter entered the house. The Holy Spirit had guided the believers to pray for Peter's safety and had rescued the leader of the early church.

5. The Holy Spirit empowers our witness

In one of the churches where my husband served as senior pastor, we had a new associate who joined the staff. He was a handsome, talented young visionary, and his preaching was quite good. But something was lacking. His preaching reached the minds, but not the hearts, of his hearers.

As he faced up to some issues in his life in which he had to trust God, a marvelous change came over him. After leaving our church, he served two churches that grew from small to extremely large. The Holy Spirit empowered his witness.

6. When we are broken or feel that we have failed, the Holy Spirit remolds us

We find a perfect example of this in Jeremiah 18:1-6. Jeremiah was sent by God to the potter's house. The potter made a marred vessel but didn't toss it into the garbage. Instead, he remolded it into a vessel of beauty. This is such a vivid example of how God can take our brokenness and remold us into something beautiful if we are willing to surrender to God's will. That scripture is put into song in the hymn "Have Thine Own Way":

> Thou art the potter; I am the clay.
> Mold me and make me after thy will,
> while I am waiting, yielded and still.
> (Adelaide A. Pollard, 1902)

The question is not how much do we have of the Holy Spirit, but how much does the Holy Spirit have of us? As we open all the rooms of our lives to his presence, we will be like a tree planted by the living waters (Psalm 1:2-3). We will bring forth fruit (Galatians 5:22-23). There is no "fruitage" without "rootage"!

When the Holy Spirit is resident within us, we not only have the fruit of the Spirit but also at least one of the spiritual gifts listed in the Scriptures. Most churches have courses on spiritual gifts, usually ending in a spiritual gift inventory. When you find your gift(s) and use them to build up the body of Christ, you will, as "the Flying Scotsman" Eric Liddell said in the movie *Chariots of Fire*, "feel the pleasure of God."

The Holy Spirit also gives each of us at least one spiritual gift to empower our living and serving. The main biblical references to spiritual gifts are Romans 12:6-8, 1 Corinthians 12:8-10, and Ephesians 4:11. God has not called a spiritually elite group. All of us have gifts, and in the words of Paul to Timothy, we need to "stir up the gift of God, which is in [us]" (2 Timothy 1:6 KJV).

A Final Word

I believe that Christianity is intelligence on fire, and the fire is the Holy Spirit resident within us. This means that Christianity is knowledge plus faith inspired by the excitement and passion of the Holy Spirit resident within us. It is just the opposite of boring or "ho-hum" faith. It is also the opposite of superstition.

On a trip to Yosemite National Park, our family learned of a traditional weekend event at the park that now is no longer practiced because of the danger of forest fires. In years past, however, on Friday and Saturday evenings at 11:00 p.m., the forest ranger would stand at the top of the falls holding a lighted torch. He would call to the tourists below, "Are you ready?"

In a loud chorus, the visitors would shout back, "We are ready! Let the fire fall!" It must have been a spectacular sight in the darkness to see the lighted torch plummeting down the cascading waters amid applause and cheers.

In a darkened world, a loving and eternal God is calling to us twenty-first–century disciples, "Are you ready to receive the fire of the Holy Spirit in your life, your church, your world?" In order to achieve happiness, peace, and power, let us say and mean, "Let the fire fall!"

Digging a Little Deeper

1. Who are the three persons of the Holy Trinity? How does each relate to body, mind, and spirit?
2. If someone asked you today to describe or explain the Holy Spirit, what would you say? What has helped you to understand who the Holy Spirit is and what the Holy Spirit does?

3. Have you, or has someone you know, ever run from God as Francis Thompson describes in his poem "The Hound of Heaven"? If so, describe the circumstances and the outcome.

4. Describe the differences among prevenient, justifying, and sanctifying grace.

5. Describe some of the ways the Holy Spirit works within us. Share one way in which you have experienced the working of the Holy Spirit in your own life.

6. Read Galatians 5:22-23. What does Paul say is the fruit of the Spirit? Which aspect of the "fruit" do you most need now? In what ways does the Holy Spirit, who indicates our need, also need our help in cultivating the fruit?

7. Read aloud Romans 12:6-8, 1 Corinthians 12:8-10, and Ephesians 4:11. What spiritual gifts are named in these verses? Are there other spiritual gifts besides these? If so, name some of them.

8. Read James 1:17 and Ephesians 4:12. From where do all gifts come? Why are we given spiritual gifts?

9. What are *your* gifts? How are you using them?

10. In what area do you most need fire (excitement and purpose) in your life, your family, your church, or your business? Open your life to the Holy Spirit, and bring zest and excitement to your living!